Christopher Columbus

CHRISTOPHER COLUMBUS

AND

THE PARTICIPATION OF THE JEWS IN THE
SPANISH AND PORTUGUESE DISCOVERIES

BY

Dr. M. KAYSERLING

TRANSLATED FROM THE AUTHOR'S MANUSCRIPT WITH HIS SANCTION
AND REVISION

By **CHARLES GROSS, Ph. D.**

Hubert Allen and Associates
Albuquerque, New Mexico, USA
2002

CHRISTOPHER COLUMBUS AND THE PARTICIPATION OF THE JEWS IN THE SPANISH AND PORTUGUESE DISCOVERIES

By Meyer Kayserling

Published by: Hubert Allen and Associates
720-25 Tramway Lane NE, Albuquerque, NM   87122   USA
2002 Edition Printed in the United States of America
2002 Edition Copyright © 2002 by Hubert A. Allen, Jr.

Publisher's Cataloging-in-Publication

Kayserling, Meyer, 1829-1905.
  [Christoph Columbus und der Anteil der Juden an den spanischen und portugiesischen Entdeckungen. English]
  Christopher Columbus and the participation of the Jews in the Spanish and Portuguese discoveries / by M. Kayserling ; translated from the author's manuscript with his sanction and revision by Charles Gross.
  p. cm.
  Includes bibliographical references and index.
  LCCN 2002103283
  ISBN 0-9641694-9-5

  1. Columbus, Christopher--Relations with Jews.
  2. America--Discovery and exploration--Spanish. 3. America --Discovery and exploration--Portuguese. 4. Jews--Spain --History. 5. Marranos. 6. Santangel, Luis de, d. 1498. 7. Spain--History--Ferdinand and Isabella, 1479-1516. I. Gross, Charles, 1857-1909, tr. II. Title.

E111.K23 2002   970.01'5
                          QBI02-701446

Modern Introduction

Meyer Kayserling (1829 - 1905) was a leading Jewish scholar in the 19th Century. His studies of Jewry in the Iberian Peninsula were largely based on original manuscripts found in the archives, libraries and private collections of Europe. His scholarship caught the eye of the Spanish government, which asked Kayserling to produce a work in honor of the 400th anniversary of the discovery of America. **"Christopher Columbus and the Participation of the Jews in the Spanish and Portuguese Discoveries"** was first published in 1894 and has been called Kayserling's most important work. Even after a century, this chronicle of the age of King Ferdinand and Queen Isabella is a fascinating and lively read.

Hubert A. Allen, Jr. , Editor/Publisher
Albuquerque, New Mexico, 2002

PREFACE.

FEW mortals have been honored by posterity as much as Christopher Columbus, though during his life-time the discoverer of a New World received little credit for his achievements. Monuments of Columbus have been erected in Genoa, proud to call him her son ; in Barcelona, where after his first voyage to America the Spanish sovereigns received him with great rejoicing and with princely honors; in Valladolid, where he died; in Seville, Madrid, Huelva, New York, San Domingo, and in many other cities of Italy, Spain, and America. His praises have been sung in odes and ballads, and his name has been glorified by dramatist and novelist.

And in our day, four hundred years after the discovery of America, his achievements have been most worthily commemorated by the academies and learned societies of all nations. To honor his name Spain has just held the great *Exposición Historico-Europea* in Madrid; and America has just closed the Chicago Exhibition, which attracted millions of visitors. The Church has canonized him. In synagogues and temples his services in promoting the social and commercial intercourse of nations, and especially in advancing nautical and geographical science, have been recognized and lauded. In the just appreciation of his great services to mankind, all political, religious, and social differences have vanished. The commemoration of his achievements has also materially enriched historical literature. His descent, his education, his voyages and discoveries, all the events of his life, have recently been investigated and described. In doing this, writers have regarded his life from different points of view. Some of his biographers have even seen in his career not the triumph of science but that of religion; and a learned Spaniard has in all seriousness asserted that without his strong religious faith Columbus would never have discovered America.* For a long time Isabella, the pious Queen of Castile, received credit for being the chief or sole promoter of his expeditions and discoveries. In recent times Aragonese writers have, however, disputed the justice of this claim, and, to maintain their national honor, have ascribed to their king, Ferdinand the Catholic, an equal share in the promotion of Columbus's plans. More or less justice has also been done to the other per-

* S. de la Rósa y López, *El Libros y Autografos de D. Chr. Colón* [Seville, 1891].

sons who helped him and who directly or indirectly participated in his discoveries.

The question whether the Jews assisted in these discoveries has already heretofore been propounded,* but it has never before been carefully investigated. The credit of having given the first impulse to the present work belongs to one of the most public-spirited citizens of America, the venerable Mr. Lazarus Straus, and to his son, Hon. Oscar S. Straus of New York, formerly minister of the United States in Turkey and since 1892 president of the American Jewish Historical Society. Entrusted with this honorable but difficult mission, I determined to visit Spain in order to complete my collection of material by exploring the Spanish archives and libraries. Such documents as I found there, I transcribed. They have been used with care in the text, and are printed *in extenso* in the Appendix *of the first edition.*†

My investigations in Spain were greatly facili-

---

* This was done thirty-six years ago by the writer of the present work in an article entitled *Die portugiesischen Entdeckungen und Eroberungen in Beziehung zu den Juden, in Monatsschrift für Geschichte und Wissenschaft des Judenthums* [Edited by Z. Frankel], vii. 433-446; *Jahrbuch für die Geschichte der Juden und des Judenthums,* vol. iii. According to C.P. Daly's *Settlement of the Jews in North America* [2d edition by M.J. Kohler, New York, 1893], Rev. Dr. Kohler delivered an address on this subject before the German Historical Society of New York ; it was printed in the *Belletristisches Journal,* May 1891.

† Editor's addition to the 2002 edition in italics.

tated by the kindness of Spanish officials and *savants*, and by the praiseworthy liberality with which the authorities of the archives at Alcalá de Henares, Barcelona, Madrid, Seville, and other places allowed me to use their manuscript treasures. My warm thanks are due particularly to certain Spanish investigators, who are well known far beyond the boundaries of Spain—to the learned and ever-obliging R. P. Fidel Fita (who has made many valuable contributions to the history of Spain), the excellent historian D. Victor Balaguer, the distinguished student of Columbus literature D. Cesáreo Fernández Duro, the amiable D. Jerónimo López de Ayala, Vizconde de Palazuelos, D. Ramón Santa María, and to several other gentlemen in Barcelona, Madrid, Seville, and Saragossa.

It only remains for me to add a few words of explanation regarding the Marranos, or secret Jews, and their status. The terrible massacres of 1391 and later persecutions had compelled or induced vast numbers of Jews to submit to baptism. The great majority of these converts adhered to Judaism more firmly than is commonly supposed. Though they had succumbed to force (*anussim*) and had become Christians in appearance or outwardly, they lived according to the precepts and laws of their ancestral faith. In the city of

Seville, a Jewish chronicle* informs us, an inquisitor thus addressed the king : "Sire, if you wish to ascertain how the *anussim,* or secret Jews, observe the Sabbath, let us ascend this tower. Behold there the house of a pseudo-Christian, yonder is another, and here are several more. However cold the weather may be, you would not see smoke rising from any of these dwellings, for it is the Sabbath, and on that day the secret Jews allow no fire to be kindled. They also have a man who slaughters animals for them according to Jewish rites and brings the meat to their houses, and another who performs circumcision."

That Jewish writers have not exaggerated the loyalty of the Marranos to their ancestral religion is proven by the countless victims of the Inquisition in Spain and Portugal and in the Spanish and Portuguese colonies who during the three centuries of its existence died in dungeons or on the funeral pile. Their religious loyalty will not be fully recognized and appreciated before the enormous mass of documentary evidence in the state archives of Alcalá de Henares and Simancas and in several archives of Portugal has been sifted and utilized. Until quite recent times this material was wholly or in great part neglected.

I trust that I have succeeded in making a

---

* Shevet Juhuda [ed. Wiener], number 64, p. 96.

contribution to the history of the discovery of America and to the history of the Jews, to whom America has been a land of refuge, a land of freedom and of equality.

M. KAYSERLING.

BUDAPEST, *October,* 1893.

CONTENTS.

CHAPTER IV.

CHAPTER V.

CHAPTER VI.

CHAPTER VII.

CONTENTS.   XV

CHAPTER VIII.

CHRISTOPHER COLUMBUS.

CHAPTER I.

THE EARLIEST PARTICIPATION OF THE JEWS IN THE NAVAL AFFAIRS OF SPAIN AND PORTUGAL—JEHUDA CRESQUES, OR JAIME RIBES—JOÃO II. AND HIS ASTRONOMICAL JUNTA.

OWING to their favorable geographical situation, Spain and Portugal early became prominent maritime powers. Their discoveries and conquests in the fifteenth and sixteenth centuries astonished the world, and turned its history into new channels. The Spaniards, particularly the people of Catalonia and Aragon, were especially active in maritime affairs. Their shipping and foreign trade developed so rapidly that they rivaled, and, in fact, soon surpassed, the mercantile marine of Venice, Pisa, and Genoa, the older commercial cities of Italy.

As early as the beginning of the thirteenth century, Barcelona's commerce with Alexandria, the capital and chief seaport of Egypt, and with the north coast of Africa, was of great importance, in spite of papal prohibitions. Even in the middle of the twelfth century the Jewish traveler Benjamin of Tudela, the predecessor of Marco Polo, mentions the prosperity of Barcelona. To inform himself concerning his co-religionists he had visited the greater part of Southern Europe, of Africa, and of Asia, and his well-known book of travels was translated into many languages. He describes Barcelona as a beautiful city, frequented by merchants from all lands—from Greece and Italy, from Egypt and Palestine, and from other neighboring parts of Asia. Ships bearing the Aragonian and Catalonian flag soon traversed the African seas, and reached Egypt and Syria. During several centuries the maritime enterprises and conquests of Aragon gave her a prominent place among the European powers.

The Jews rendered noteworthy services in connection with the marine development of Spain. R. Jehuda of Valencia, or, as he was called by contemporary historians, Don Jehudano, the richest Jew of Aragon, was the confidential friend and the treasurer of King Jaime I., who asked his advice in the most important affairs of state. In 1263, at the request of the king, he fitted out a fleet which was placed in command of the Infante Don Fernando Sanchez, and three years later Jehuda was intrusted with the preparations for the conquest of Murcia.* In 1323, when Don Alfonso, the heir-apparent of the crown of Aragon, fitted out a great fleet for the conquest of Cerdeña, Tortosa showed more patriotic zeal than any other city in the kingdom. The rich Jewish community of that town, at its own expense, equipped and manned two galleys. Before the fleet sailed, King Jaime II. assured the Jews of Tortosa of his gratitude and good-will.† Moreover, the Jews of Aragon soon participated in maritime affairs personally, as well as financially. To mention only one example, Juceff Faquin, a Jew of Barcelona, "had navigated the whole then known world," as King Jaime III., the last king of Mallorca, himself testifies in 1334.‡

As in Aragon, so also in Castile the Jews contributed to the development of the navy. When King Sancho IV. formed a plan to wrest Tarifa from the Moors, he found that he had not money enough to equip his fleet. In this emergency Don Juda, treasurer of the queen Maria de Molina, lent him twenty thousand maravedis in gold. Without this assistance the king could not have

---

* Tourtoulon, *Jacme I. le Conquérant*, liv. 4, cap. 3; Balaguer, *Historia de Cataluña*, liv. 6, cap. 12; *Archivo de la Corona de Aragon*, Reg. 12, fol. 17.

† Balaguer, liv. 7, cap. II ; *Archivo de la Corona de Aragon*, Reg. 224, fol. 119.

‡ *Revue des Études Juives*, iv. 53 sq.

undertaken the expedition, and it would have been   necessary   to postpone the conquest of Tarifa.*

The first ruler of Portugal who promoted the development of a navy was Sancho II., whose reign marks the beginning of that country's maritime activity. The   Jews of the kingdom were soon required   to furnish an anchor, and a new cable sixty ells long, for every new ship fitted out by the crown (the so-called "fleet-tax"); and, already in early times, they were employed in the naval service.†   Under King João I. discoveries and   conquests began along the African coast. Cueta, the seven-hilled city, the most important fortress of Mauritania, was captured in 1415, and thus the end was attained for which fame-loving princes of Portugal had long and ardently sought. On the armada which   was sent to take the city, and   which left Lisbon amid the plaudits of the whole population, there were also Jews, one of whom heroically died for his country in a naval engagement.‡

João I.'s third son Henry, called the Navigator,

---

* J. Amador de los Rios, *Historia de los Judios de España y Portugal* [Madrid, 1876], ii. 61.

† Ribeiro, *Dissert.*, iii. 2, 87 sq. ; Kayserling, *Gesch. der Juden in Portugal*, 55.

‡ *Chron. do Conde D. Pedro*, in *Collecção de livros ineditos da Historia Portugueza* [Lisbon, 1790], ii. 259.

had accompanied his father on the expedition against Ceuta. After the capture of the city he obtained information from Jewish travellers concerning the south coast of Guinea and the interior of Africa. This information convinced him that valuable discoveries could be made along the African coast, and that here a new route to the land of the legendary Christian king, Prester John, could be found. In his zeal to acquire new possessions for Portugal, he devoted himself wholly to navigation, and he applied himself assiduously to nautical studies. He desired, above all, to provide for the thorough education of navigators, and hence he established a naval academy, or school of navigation, at the Villa do Iffante, or Sagres, a seaport town which he had caused to be built. To this school he called the most distinguished nautical scholars of his time, and appointed as its director Mestre Jaime of Mallorca.

Alexander von Humboldt in his *Cosmos* asks, Who was this Mestre Jaime? He was not Jaime Ferrer, the discoverer of Rio del Oro, as writers long supposed. Our Mestre Jaime, or James, early gained the reputation of a great mathematician, and was very skilful in the manufacture of maps and nautical instruments.* His real name was

---

* " Mestre Jacome, homem mui docto na arte de navegar, que fazia cartas e instrumentos." Barros, *Asia,* dec. I, cap. 16.

Jafuda or Jehuda Cresques. He was the son of Abraham Cresques of Palma, the capital of Mallorca, which since the thirteenth century had been the chief seat of nautical knowledge. Here, in the home of Raymond Lull, whose *Arte de Navagar,* even in Columbus's time, was considered the best nautical treatise, cartography was a special object of study; and, as Gabriel Llabrés y Quintana, the learned vice-president of the *Luliana* in Palma, states, it was almost entirely in the hands of the Mallorcan Jews.

Jafuda Cresques was so prominent in this art, to which he had devoted himself from early youth, that the people called him *lo jueu buscoler* or *el judio de las brujelas,* "the map-Jew" or "the compass-Jew," just as his friend Moses Rimos, or Raymundo Barthomeu,* was popularly known as *el pergaminero,* the "parchment-maker." The maps of Jafuda Cresques were highly prized, not merely by navigators, but also by kings, and princes. Juan I. of Aragon obtained from him a map of the world, which the king esteemed so much that he assigned a room in his palace at Barcelona for

---

* He may be identical with the Moses Rimos mentioned in Steinschneider's *Catal. MSS. Biblioth. Reg. Monachensis,* p.36, who bought a Hebrew book in 1371. He was a kinsman of Moses Rimos, the physician and poet, who died in Sicily, at the age of twenty-four, in 1430.

its custody ; and when he desired to make a present to the ruler of France, he could think of nothing more costly than this map, which is still preserved as a precious relic in the National Library in Paris. In 1387 King Juan obtained another *mapa mundi* from Jafuda at the then high price of sixty-eight pounds.*

The celebrated cosmographer, the maker of the renowned *Cataluña,* lived peacefully in his stately house in Mount Zion Street, quite near to the synagogue of Palma, until August, 2 1391, when a riot broke out which soon assumed the character of an open revolt. The furious mob attacked the Jews, who had no presentiment of impending evil, and, before the governor of the island could interfere, three hundred of them were slain. Eight hundred took refuge in the royal castle or in the university, while many others fled to the churches and were baptized. Jehuda Cresques, assuming the name of Jaime Ribes, sold his house, left the island, and by virtue of privileges granted to him by the king, with whom he stood in high favor, he settled in Barcelona, the dwelling-place of

---

* G.Llabrés y Quintana, *Boletin de la sociedad arqueológica Lu-liana,* 1890, p. 310; *Boletin de la real Academia de la Historia en Madrid,* xix. 375 sq. See also Hamy, *Cresques le Juheu, note sur un géographe juif catalan de la fin du xiv. siècle* [Paris, 1891]. Hasdai Cresques should not be confused with Jafuda Cresques.

several of his relatives—Jafuda Lobell Cresques, Solomon and Azay Cresques, and others. Here he continued to devote himself to his art, receiving employment from such persons as King Martin of Aragon, until 1438. In that year, when nearly sixty years old, he was appointed by Prince Henry director of the newly established academy at Sagres, with a large salary. This was the academy in which was laid the foundation of Columbus's projects. Mestre Jaime became the teacher of the Portuguese in the art of navigation as well as in the manufacture of nautical instruments and maps. In this work he had no superior in his day. To him we are chiefly indebted for the improvement of the compass and for the application of the astronomical astrolabe to navigation.[*]

From Henry the Navigator, who lived to hear of the discovery of Cape Verd and the Azores, his grand-nephew João II., who became King of Portugal in 1481, seems to have inherited a love of exploration. His attention was constantly occupied with nautical affairs ; he desired, above

---

[*] Barros, *Asia,* dec. I, cap. 16 : "D. Henrique mandou vir Mestre Jacome, o qual lhe custou muito, pelo trazer en este Reyno pero insinar sua sciencia aos officiaes portuguezes." Candido Lusitano, *Vida do Infante D. Henrique* [Lisbon, 1758], 196 sq. ; *Os Portuguezes em Africa, Asia e Oceania* [Lisbon, 1877], i. 12.

all, to provide navigators with mathematical instruments for the determination of latitude and longitude. The astrolabe, to the development of which Jewish scholars such as Abraham Ibn Esra, the physician Jacob ben Machir (also called Don Profatius), Jacob Carsoni, and others had contributed, was still imperfect; an instrument was needed by means of which the distance of a ship from the equator could be exactly computed by the varying position of the sun in the different seasons. King João requested his astronomical junta to devise some means by which navigators might, with some degree of certainty, direct their course in any part of the ocean, and thus prevent their vessels from going astray. This junta, or commission, consisted of Diogo Ortiz Castellano, Bishop of Ceuta, who acted as president, Mestre Joseph, or Joseph Vecinho,* the court physician Rodrigo, the mathematician Moses, and the Nuremberg navigator and cosmographer Martin Behaim. An epoch in the progress of nautical knowledge was made by the improvement of the astrolabe, and by the invention of a means of determining the meridian altitude of the sun—an invention by which later discoveries were facilitated and perhaps rendered possible. These

---

* Vecinho was the king's physician, an excellent mathematician and cosmographer, a pupil of Abraham Zacuto.

improvements were in great part due, as most writers admit, to Portuguese Jews.* From the middle of the fifteenth century the Portuguese were considered the foremost navigators of the world, and their discoveries evoked general admiration. King João gladly received and patronized foreign navigators, and all who were versed in nautical affairs or in cosmography.

---

* Barros, *Asia,* dec. I. liv. 3, cap. 2; Telles Sylvius, *De rebus gestis Johannis II.,* 90 ; Maffei, *Historia Indiarum,* 51 ; *Mem. d. Litt. Portugueza,* viii. 163.

CHAPTER II.

IN 1472 a young Genoese, twenty-six years of age, proceeded to the capital of Portugal, hoping to find there the best outlet for his nautical zeal and the most rapid advancement in a maritime career. It was Cristoforo Colombo, or, to use the Latin form, Christophorus Columbus, who, after settling in Spain, called himself Colón.

Born in 1446, Columbus was the son of a poor weaver of Genoa. He spent his youth in Savona, a small maritime town, in which, as in Genoa, several Jewish families dwelt in mediæval seclusion. He and his brothers helped their father in his work, but soon Columbus followed his natural inclination, and devoted himself to navigation. Concerning his boyhood days and his education we have little authentic information; there is no historical evidence that he enjoyed the advantages of higher education, or that he attended the University of Pavia.

In 1472 we find him in Lisbon. Here, a few years later, he married Felipa Moñiz, whose grandfather was not, as some assert, of Jewish stock. Columbus was a skilful cartographer and draughtsman. He supported himself by drawing maps, in which he also dealt, just as later, in Andalusia, he traded in printed books. He was no stranger to the Jews of Lisbon. Whether he had intimate commercial relations with them, or whether in his frequent financial troubles he obtained assistance from any of them, it is difficult to determine. But we know that in his will he requested that "a half mark in silver should be paid to a Jew dwelling at the gate of the Jewry, or to him whom a priest would designate."[*] Long before Columbus made his will the Jews had disappeared from Lisbon.

" I have had constant relations," he himself says, " with many learned men, clergy and laymen, Jews and Moors, and many others."[†] He had personal intercourse with Martin Behaim, who was about the same age as Columbus, also with Joseph Vecinho (the above-mentioned mathema-

---

* " A un Judio que moraba á la puerta de la Juderia en Lisboa, ó á quien mandare un sacerdote el valor de medio marco de plata." Navarrete, *Coleccion de los Viages y Descubrimientos,* ii. 313; *Coleccion de Documentos inéditos de España,* xvi. 424 sq.

† *Libro de las Profecias,* fol. iv.

tician and royal physician), and with other learned Jews of Lisbon. Vecinho prepared a translation of Zacuto's astronomical tables, and gave a copy to Columbus, who, as we shall see, carried it on his travels and found it of very great service.*

During his sojourn of several years in Lisbon, which was interrupted by journeys to the coast of Guinea, Columbus worked very industriously and perseveringly to add to his meagre knowledge of mathematics and geography. In order to carry out the ambitious plans which he had formed, he devoted his attention to cosmography, philosophy, history, and similar subjects; several of his biographers say that he studied Aristotle and Duns Scotus, Pliny and Strabo, Josephus and Chronicles, the Church Fathers and the Arabian writings of the Jews. We are naturally led to inquire, What were his favorite works? What books were really in his possession?

The treatises which he studied with most zeal were Æneas Sylvius's *Historia rerum ubique gestarum* and Bishop Pierre d'Ailly's *Imago Mundi.* This latter work, it may be incidentally observed, had already in the fourteenth century been translated into Hebrew. Columbus's knowledge of

---

* It was afterwards found in his library. *Biblioteca Colombina con notas del Dr. D. Simón de la Rosa y López* [Seville, 1888], i. 3.

Aristotle, Strabo, Seneca, and other Latin and Greek classics was derived from Pierre d'Ailly's book; the *Imago Mundi* was his constant traveling companion, and his copy of it is filled with his own marginal annotations. Besides Zacuto's astronomical tables, already mentioned, he possessed some of the works written by or ascribed to Abraham Ibn Esra; for example, the little book on the "Critical Days," *Liber de luminaribus et diebus criticis,* and the *De Nativitatibus.** Ibn Esra was an eminent man of learning; his name was honored by Christians as well as Jews. Zacuto doubtless called Columbus's attention to the *De Nativitatibus* during the latter's residence in Salamanca ; he bought a copy of it in that city, according to a note in his own handwriting, for forty-one maravedis.† Later, in Spain, he read with religious zeal the tract on the Messiah, which was written by the proselyte Samuel Ibn Abbas of Morocco for the purpose of converting R. Isaac of Sujurmente; it had been translated into Spanish in 1339, and into Latin a hundred years later. This book interested Columbus so much that he excerpted

---

* It was printed in Venice in 1485 : *De Nativitatibus al reverso de la hoja primera con circulo dividido en grados y con lineas geometricas.*   Venetiis, A ° MCCCCLXXXV, nona Kalend. Januarii.

† These books are now in the Colombina at Seville.   See *Biblioteca Colombina, i. 3.*

three whole chapters.* He was also very fond of reading the Bible and the Fourth Book of Ezra, which was probably written by a Jew who lived outside of Palestine. According to his own assertion, the incentive that impelled him to plan his discoveries was not a love of science, but his interpretation of the prophecies of Isaiah.

In Portugal Columbus earnestly conceived the idea of making maritime discoveries by way of the west. He wished to find a new ocean route to the regions of Cathay and Cipango, which were reputed to be rich in gold and spices; and also to the realm of the priest-king John, whose letter to Pope Eugene IV., or to Emperor Frederick III., a Jew is said to have first published in the middle of the fifteenth century. Henry the Navigator had already conceived a similar plan, and the Portuguese kings never lost sight of it. This bold conception took firm root in the mind of Columbus, mainly through a letter which the great Florentine physician and astrologer Toscanelli sent to King João through the monk

---

* *Libro de las Profecias,* fol. 13, in Navarrete, *Coleccion de los Viages,* ii. 260 sq.; *R. Semuel Israel [Ismael] oriundus de Civitate regis morochorum ad R. Isaac Magistrum Synagogæ quæ est in Subjulmeta, trasl. de hebreo vel de arabico in lat. p. Franc. Alfonsum Boni-Hominis, Hispanum ord. Predicatorum* [1438]. It was originally written in Arabic.

Fernando Martinez. Columbus applied to Toscanelli for a copy of this letter, and received it through Girardi, a Genoese, who was then living in Lisbon. Columbus at length proceeded to carry out his project. He laid before King João a proposition to lead a squadron along the African coast, and thence across the ocean to the land whose wealth Marco Polo had so misleadingly described. The sullen, distrustful monarch regarded Columbus as a visionary babbler, and, especially on account of the navigator's enormous demands, saw in his scheme more pride than truth. But João laid the matter before his nautical junta, consisting of Diogo Ortiz, Bishop of Ceuta, and the court physicians Joseph and Rodrigo. They regarded the project as chimerical, and said that the whole plan rested on Columbus's visionary conception of Marco Polo's Island of Cipango.* Nevertheless the king considered the matter of such importance that he submitted it for further consideration to his council of state, in which Pedro de Menezes, Count of Villa-Real, exercised a dominant influence. Menezes thought that the exploration of the

---

* " El Rey porque via ser este Christovão Colon . . . mandou que estivesse com D. Diogo Ortiz, Bispo do Ceuta, e com mestre Rodrigo e mestre Josepe, a quem elle commetia estas cousas da cosmografia." Barros, *Asia,* dec. I, liv. 3, cap. II.

African coast would be more conducive to the interests of Portugal, and hence he advised the king
not to be misled by the vision of Columbus. In
a long speech the count dwelt upon his reasons
for giving this advice. His arguments were based
mainly on the views of JosephVecinho, who was
his as well as the king's physician, and whom he
regarded as the highest authority in nautical
matters.*

The ruler of Portugal finally refused to assist
Columbus in his plans of exploration; or, as
Columbus expressed it in May, 1505, in a letter
to Ferdinand of Aragon, God had so stricken the
king with blindness that during fourteen years he
could not perceive what was desired of him.† The
explorer was greatly exasperated by João's refusal,
and his anger was particularly directed against
"the Jew Joseph," to whom he attributed the
chief blame in the miscarriage of his plans. His
manuscript notes in the Colombina in Seville mention Vicinho twice. In these passages Columbus
states that the King of Portugal sent his "physician and astrologer" Joseph to measure the altitude of the sun throughout Guinea, and that " the

---

* "Mestre Josepe . . . a que o Conde dava grande authori-
dade." Ruy de Pina, *Chron. do Conde D. Duarte,* in *Collecção de
livros ineditos,* iii. 54.

† Navarrete, *Coleccion de los Viages,* iii. 528.

Jew Joseph " gave an account of this mission to the king in the presence of Christopher's brother Bartholomew and many others ; probably Columbus himself was also present.*

Portugal did not, however, abandon the hope of finding an ocean route to India, even without foreign aid. The wily, parsimonious king wished to turn Columbus's plans to account, without conceding any of the latter's demands. Hence, in May, 1487, he sent to the Levant two knights of his court, Affonso de Payva and Pedro de Covilhão. They departed from Lisbon with orders to seek information concerning India and the kingdom of Prester John, and they were intrusted with letters to this monarch from the Portuguese ruler. Affonso de Payva took the route to Ethiopia, and proceeded along the African coast to Sambaya, in company with a Jewish merchant whom he met on the way. The two soon be-

---

* Columbus's manuscript note in Æneas Sylvius's *Historia rerum ubique gestarum* [Venice, 1477], p. 25: "Nota quod serenissimus rex portugaliæ misit in guineam anno domini 1485 *Josephum fixicum ejus et astrologum* ad capiendum altitudinem solis in tota guinea, qui omnia adimplevit et renuntiavit dicto serenissimo regi *me presente* cum multis aliis in die xi. marcii." Manuscript note in Pierre d'Ailly's *De imagine mundi,* p. 42: "Luego proximante a Março de 1485 cuando *el judio Josepho* hacia relacion al Rey acerca del resultado de su comision, D. Bartholomeo se hallo presente en este acto."

came intimate friends, and De Payva confided to his companion the object of his journey. Soon after their arrival in Ormuz he was stricken with a fatal illness, to the great sorrow of his Jewish friend, who solemnly promised the dying man to return to Lisbon and give the king an accurate account of all they had learned on their journey. The Jew faithfully kept his word.[*]

Pedro de Covilhão, for whom, at the king's command, Vecinho and Rodrigo had prepared a terrestrial globe,[†] visited Goa, Calicut, and Aden, and pushed onward as far as Sofala, on the east coast of South Africa. He then returned to Cairo, where he and De Payva had agreed to meet. Here he found two Jews from Portugal awaiting him, the learned Abraham of Beja and Joseph Zapateiro of Lamego. They brought the knight letters and orders from the king. Joseph had formerly visited Bagdad, and when he returned to Portugal he informed King João of what he had learned concerning Ormuz, the chief emporium for the spices of India. João requested him and the linguist Abraham to go in search of the errant Covilhão, and to direct him to send to Lisbon, through Joseph, news concerning the success of his expedition ; and there-

---

* *Collecção de Documentos ineditos para a Historia das Conquistas dos Portuguezes* [Lisbon, 1858], i. 6.
† Mariz, *Dialogos,* dial. 4, cap. 10, p. 315.

after, in company with Abraham, to secure accurate information about affairs in Ormuz. Accordingly, Joseph Zapateiro joined a caravan whose goal was Aleppo, and carried back to Portugal all the information that Covilhão had gathered from Indian and Arabian mariners. The knight informed the king that, by proceeding along the west coast, the Portuguese could without difficulty reach the southern extremity of Africa. But before Joseph arrived at his destination, it was already known in Lisbon that Bartholomew Diaz had not merely discovered, but had also doubled, Cabo Tormentoso, the Cape of Good Hope.*

After his offers had been rejected by the king, Columbus resolved to leave Portugal, hoping to secure assistance elsewhere for the execution of his plans—in Genoa, in Venice, or from the King of France. His situation was indeed most wretched. He had lost his wife ; he was poor, and was daily pressed by his creditors, so that he had to depart from Lisbon secretly, at night, with his little son Diego. He left Portugal in 1484, and proceeded towards Huelva, where he intended to place his child in charge of his wife's married sister. After trying in vain to induce Enrique de Guzman, the Duke of Medina-Sidonia, to co-operate with him in his projects of discovery, he

---

* Garcia de Resende, *Chron. del Rey D. João II.,* fol. 29.

applied to Luis de la Cerda, the first Duke of Medina-Celi, one of the richest princes of Andalusia. Luis, in whose veins Jewish blood flowed (his grandmother was of Jewish stock*), received him hospitably, kept him in his place for a long time,† and seemed inclined to undertake the expedition at his own expense, especially as Columbus demanded only three or four thousand ducats in order to secure two caravels. To equip ships it was necessary, however, to obtain the assent of the crown, but permission was refused. Then the duke wrote from Rota to the queen, and on his recommendation, Columbus, after a long delay, secured access to the Spanish sovereigns, Ferdinand of Aragon and Isabella of Castile.

---

* *El Tizon de la Nobleza Española* [Barcelona, n. d.], 71.

† There is no proof that Columbus was the duke's guest for two years, as his biographers assert. In the duke's letter to the Cardinal of Spain, he says : " Yo tuve en mi casa *mucho tiempo* á C. Colón."

CHAPTER III.

COLUMBUS sought his fortune at the Spanish court during a period of violent political revolutions. It was not an opportune time for him to secure aid for his enterprise from the rulers of Spain. Discord prevailed in Castile and Aragon, in Catalonia and Navarre, and war raged along the southern frontier of the Iberian Peninsula. Under the amiable but impotent King Henry IV., Castile had been in a condition of anarchy. On every side plots were formed by turbulent grandees, dissatisfied with the king and with his government. The crown was impoverished ; even in the royal palace the most pressing wants often remained unsatisfied. The conduct of the pleasure-loving queen evoked all kinds of rumors. Beltran de la Cueva was her favorite, and the people called her daughter Beltraneja. The king, who had long been a constant object of ridicule, was at length dethroned, and his brother Alfonso was proclaimed his successor (1465).

The situation was not much better in the lands over which Juan II. of Aragon ruled. Catalonia was in arms; Aragon was threatened with the outbreak of a revolt; Navarre was the scene of bloody conflicts occasioned by the king's own son, Carlos de Viana, who claimed the right to rule on the ground that he was his mother's heir. After the death of his first wife, who was a French princess, King Juan, at the age of fifty, had married Juana Enriquez, the daughter of Fadrique Enriquez, Admiral of Castile. She was the grandchild of the beautiful Paloma, a Jewess of Toledo, and she bore the king a son, Ferdinand, whom historians call the Catholic.* To secure her son the succession to the throne, Queen Juana, a woman of virile strength and intrepid spirit, did all in her power to prejudice the king against Carlos de Viana, of whom the people were very fond; indeed, Juan, in compliance with the wish of the Catalonian cortes, intended to declare Don Carlos his successor. But Juana persuaded the king that the prince was conspiring against his life and

---

* *De Vita et Scriptis Eliæ Kapsali . . . acced. Excerpta ad Judeorum historiam pertinentia ex MS. Kapsalii Historia* [Padua, 1869], p. 58. The manuscript of Kapsali's chronicle is in the Ambrosiana in Milan.

crown, and that, by marrying Isabella of Castile, he intended to form a coalition with the latter's brother, Henry IV. Don Carlos was soon gotten rid of by poison, and an open revolt against the crown then broke out.

King Juan's most loyal adherents were the Jews, and they rendered him important services. For example, the skill of Abiatar Aben Crescas, his court physician and astrologer, restored his eyesight. The king exhibited so much liberality and good-will towards the Jews that his death caused them profound grief. Several Jewish communities of the kingdom assembled at Cervera to hold a memorial service ; they sang Hebrew psalms and Spanish funeral songs, and Aben Crescas delivered a eulogy on the character of the good monarch.[*]

Juan's long-cherished hope to unite Aragon and Castile was virtually realized before he died. In 1469 his son Ferdinand married Isabella of Castile, Henry IV.'s sister, who, after the death of her brother Alfonso, had been recognized as his successor, and had been proclaimed ruler of Castile, though she did not really succeed to the throne until after the death of Henry IV. in 1474. The accomplishment of this marriage was materially promoted by Jews and Marranos, for it was as-

---

[*] Balaguer, *Historia de Cataluña,* lib. 17, cap. 27.

sumed that Ferdinand would, like his father, be friendly towards the Jews, especially as he himself had inherited Jewish blood from his mother. Don Abraham Senior was particularly prominent in the matrimonial negotiations. He was a rich Jew of Segovia, who, owing to his sagacity, his eminent services, and his position as the king's chief farmer of taxes, exerted great influence. He urged the grandees of Castile to support the proposed marriage between the Princess Isabella, who had many suitors, and the distinguished Ferdinand of Aragon, who was already King of Sicily, and who, even in his early youth, had displayed much valor. Although Don Abraham met with violent opposition from a part of the Castilian nobility, he induced the prince to make a secret journey to Toledo. Isabella, who was favorably inclined toward her cousin of Aragon, readily agreed to a meeting. Ferdinand started on the journey without delay. Being destitute of means, he secured a loan of twenty thousand sueldos from his "beloved servant," Jaime Ram, the son of a rabbi, and one of the most distinguished jurists of his time.* Ferdinand then crossed the frontier of

---

* In 1474, Ferdinand ordered his treasurer to repay the twenty thousand sueldos to his "amado criado" Jaime Ram. The document, dated Caceres, March 10, 1474, is in the *Arch. de la Corona de Aragon,* Reg. 3633, fol. 80 dorse.

Castile in disguise, and found shelter in the house
of Abraham Senior, who took him quietly at night
to the expectant princess.*

Pedro de la Caballeria, a very rich and distinguished young Marrano of Saragossa, a member
of a family with many branches, was then entrusted with the task of winning over persons of
rank who opposed the marriage project—Alfonso
Carillo, the fickle Archbishop of Toledo, Pedro
Gonzales de Mendoza, Bishop of Siguenza, who
later became Cardinal of Spain, and others. By
his power of persuasion, and by the extensive
resources at his disposal, he, in fact, contrived
that Ferdinand should be preferred to the King
of Portugal, the Duke of Berri, the King of England, and all of Isabella's other suitors. Pedro de
la Caballeria also had the distinguished honor of
presenting to the royal bride, as Ferdinand's nup-
tial gift, a costly necklace valued at forty thousand ducats, and of paying the whole or a large
part of its cost. The crown of Aragon was, in fact,
so impoverished in those days that, on the death
of King Juan, in 1479, jewels had to be taken from
the treasury and sold, in order to bury him with
such obsequies as were appropriate to royalty.†

---

* Kapsali, op. cit., 60 sq. ; Mariana, De Rebus Hispaniæ, lib.
24, cap. I.

† Zurita, Anales de Aragon, iv. 165.

Abraham Senior, the intimate friend of the influential Andreas de Cabrera of Segovia, remained Isabella's most loyal adherent. He and Cabrera succeeded in effecting a reconciliation between her and her brother King Henry. Abraham stood so high in the esteem of the queen and the grandees that, in 1480, the cortes in Toledo, in recognition of his eminent services to the state, granted him a yearly stipent of ten thousand maravedis out of the revenues of the royal taxes.*

In Castile, as well as in Aragon, certain Jews, and especially many Marranos, wielded considerable influence. The name "Marrano" was applied to persons of Jewish stock whose parents or grandparents had been driven by despair and dire persecution to accept Christianity. The conversion was, however, only external, or feigned; at heart they adhered loyally to their ancestral religion. Though outwardly Christians, they secretly observed the tenets of the Jewish faith ; this was not infrequently true even in the case of those who had become dignitaries of the Church. They celebrated the sabbath and holidays, assembled in subterranean or other secret synagogues, and practiced Jewish rites in their homes. They thus remained Jews, and eventually they suf-

---

* *Coleccion de Documentos inéditos para la Historia de España,* xiii. 196.

fered torture and torments for their adhesion to Judaism.* The people and the rulers knew all this, but for a long time the Marranos were not molested, because, though they generally married within their own class, their family alliances extended into the highest strata of society. Their services were, moreover, regarded as indispensable. By their wealth, intelligence, and ability, they obtained the most important offices and positions of trust; they were employed in the cabinets of rulers, in the administration of the finances, in the higher law-courts, and in the cortes.

Though Ferdinand and Isabella were united by marriage, each had the guidance of a separate kingdom, so that they lived like two allied monarchs. They had not merely separate kingdoms, but also separate administrations and separate royal councils. The most important positions in these councils were held by Marranos—members of the families of De la Caballeria, Sanchez, Santangel, and others. Just as Luis de la Caballeria, the son of Don Bonafos, had been the confidant of King Juan of Aragon, so Jaime de la Caballeria, the brother of Luis, was the confidential friend of Ferdinand. Jaime accompanied him on his first journey to Naples, and constantly attended him with all the pomp of a prince. Alfonso, an-

---

* Kapsali, *op. cit.*, 56.

other brother of Luis, occupied the high position of Vice-Chancellor of Aragon, and Martin de la Caballeria was commander of the fleet at Mallorca. Luis Sanchez, a son of the rich Eleasar Usuf of Saragossa, was appointed president of the highest tribunal of Aragon; Gabriel Sanchez was chief treasurer, and his brother Alfonso was deputy-treasurer. Guillen Sanchez, Ferdinand's cup-bearer, was later promoted to the office of royal treasurer, and his brother Francisco was made steward of the royal household. Ferdinand also appointed Francisco Gurrea, Gabriel Sanchez's son-in-law, governor of Aragon. Whenever Ferdinand needed money he applied to the Santangels, who had commercial houses in Calatayud, Saragossa, and Valencia; of this family more will be said later. The Marranos Miguel de Almazan and Gaspar de Berrachina, the son of Abiatar Xamos, were the king's private secretaries.

In the cities, in the administration of public revenues, in the army, judiciary, and cortes, the Marranos, as has already been intimated, held important and influential offices. They were particularly prominent in Saragossa; this was the richest city of Aragon, owing to its extensive industries, which were largely conducted by Jews and Marranos. In Saragossa the Marrano Pedro Monfort was vicar-general of the archbishopric ;

Juan Cabrero was archdeacon ; and the priors of the cathedral were Dr. Lopez, a grandson of Mayer Pazagon of Calatayud, and Juan Artal, a grandson of Pedro de Almazan. One of the chief bailiffs of Saragossa was Pedro de la Cabra, a son of the Jew Nadassan Malmerca. Not less influential than in Aragon and at the Aragonese court were the Marranos who enjoyed the confidence of Queen Isabella. Her privy councillors and private secretaries were sons and grandsons of Jews ; even her confessor, Hernando de Talavera, was the grandson of a Jewess.

The fact that the Marranos, whose number in the whole of Spain was very large, possessed great wealth and were everywhere esteemed for their intelligence, aroused envy and hatred. The fact that they also loyally adhered to their ancestral religion and had active intercourse with the Jews, disturbed the fanatic portion of the Spanish clergy. In 1478, the same year in which Muley Abul Hasan received the Spanish ambassador for the last time, in the most magnificent chamber of the Alhambra, and renounced the Spanish tribute, there assembled in Seville a number of clergymen, most of them Dominicans. Isabella was temporarily residing in that city, and she presided over the meeting. Its object was to determine what could be done to fortify and invigorate the Christian faith, especially among the Marranos. The clergy tried to convince the queen that the ordinary means of conversion, recommended by her, remained ineffective in the case of the New Christians, who did not believe in the fundamental doctrines of Christianity, but tenaciously clung to Judaism. Hence the assembly recommended the introduction of the Inquisition in the form in which it already existed in Sicily. Ferdinand, who in his boundless avarice and insatiable greed was always guided by considerations of self-interest and egoism, gladly accepted the proposition.

It has long been known, and Spanish historians of the present day freely admit, that the introduction of the Inquisition was due not so much to religious zeal as to material considerations ; it was used as an instrument of avarice and of political absolutism. One aim of the power-loving king was to humble and subdue the Castilian nobles, who possessed great privileges, and among whom were not a few Marranos. His chief object was, however, to secure the wealth of the Marranos. A conflict with the Moors was inevitable ; the signal of war had already been given. The royal treasury was empty. The people were already overburdened with taxes, and even the clergy were taxed, a thing that had never before happened in Spain. The king regarded the introduction of the

Inquisition, and the confiscation of the property of its victims, as the only available method of improving the desperate financial situation. Already in the cortes of 1465 certain extremists had proposed to prosecute the secret Jews, and to use their property in carrying on a war of extermination against the Moors. This project was executed fifteen years later by Ferdinand. As soon as the first tribunal of the Inquisition was established, Fernando Yaños de Lobon was ordered to transfer to the royal treasury the property of all condemned Jews.* The Inquisition enabled the king to satisfy his ambition fully. Just as Ferdinand, who was a dissembling bigot rather than a devout Christian, always talked religion, so he always commended peace, although he really desired to conquer the Moors, and to declare war against France after Louis XI.'s death. He, the ruler of a small kingdom, wished to become the head of a great state ; the grandchild of the Toledan Jewess wrapped himself in the mantle of piety in order to elevate himself to the position of the most Catholic king.

The pious Isabella, who disliked to glorify religion at the expense of humanity, long opposed the

---

* "El Lic^do Fernand Yaños de Lobon, Adelantaide de Casa i Corte va comisiado para cobrar los bienes de los Judios que han seido e fueron condenados por los inquisidores." *Arch. de Sevilla, Libro de Cartas de 1480,* fol. 5, *Coleccion Muñoz* (Bibl. de la Academia de la Historia en Madrid).

introduction of the Inquisition, but she finally yielded to the exhortations of her exalted prelates and to the urgent solicitations of her husband. She was the pliant tool of spiritual advisors, who exercised unrestricted dominion over her, and virtually made her their slave. When, for example, she requested her confessor, Hernando de Talavera, who later became Archbishop of Granada, to allow her to confess either standing or sitting, he refused both alternatives, and insisted that she, the queen, should kneel at his feet. She yielded to his demand without a word of protest. It was entirely due to her that the Inquisition did not begin its horrible work until two years after permission for its establishment in Castile had been granted by the pope.

It is not our purpose to consider in detail the history of this institution with its cruel tortures, its scandalous procedure, and its thousands of victims. In composing such a history the pen must be dipped in blood and tears, and the writer should turn to account the great mass of unprinted material preserved in the state archives at Alcalá de Henares, most of which has never been utilized.*

---

* I intend, at no distant date, to write a history of the Spanish Inquisition, with special reference to the *Judaizantes,* or Judaizers, for which there is abundant material in the state archives of Alcalá de Henares, Seville, and elsewhere.

We have to examine merely the early operations of the Inquisition, and to call attention briefly to the victims belonging to those families whose members figure prominently in later chapters of this book. The first tribunal was established at Seville. The first inquisitors entered that city in the beginning of January, 1481, and a few days later the first victims died at the stake. Several of the richest and most respected men of Seville were soon consigned to the flames—Diego de Suson, who possessed a fortune of ten million sueldos, and who had some repute as a Talmudist, Juan Abolafia, who had been for several years farmer of the royal customs, Manuel Sauli, and others. Several thousand persons, mainly rich Marranos, perished at the stake in Seville and Cadiz in 1481. Even the bones of those who had died long before were exhumed and burned, and the property of their heirs was ruthlessly confiscated by the state. Tribunals were soon established at Cordova, Jaen, and Ciudad-Real. The bull issued by Pope Sixtus IV., October 17, 1483, appointed the blood-thirsty Torquemada inquisitor-general, and allowed Ferdinand to extend the Inquisition to the hereditary lands of his house—Aragon, Catalonia, and Valencia. In this last province it had begun a year before, at the king's special command, to confiscate the property of the Marranos.* In the cities the introduction of the Holy Office met with violent opposition. The citizens of Teruel would not allow the inquisitors to perform their noxious work. When they approached Plasencia the members of the municipal council left the city. Barcelona feared that the new tribunal would be injurious to trade. The Aragonese, jealous of their old chartered rights, observed with profound dismay that the Inquisition was making their country dependent on Castile ; they apprehended that this institution would cause the destruction of their ancient freedom.

In Aragon an arrangement for its introduction was made with the cortes, whose consent was necessary. The concurrence of that body was secured through the direct influence of Ferdinand and Isabella, both of whom had proceeded to Saragossa for that purpose. But scarcely had the two inquisitors, the Canon Pedro Arbués and the Dominican Gaspar Juglar, begun their work when they met with strong resistance. The opposition increased after the first *auto-de-fe,* and after proceedings had been begun against Leonardo or Samuel de Eli, one of the richest men of Saragossa.

---

* Pragmática de 12 Mai, 1482. *Libros de Credes e Ordinaciones (Arch. Municipal de Barcelona).*

Hence the states-general of the kingdom, having been summoned by Alfonso de la Caballeria, resolved to send a deputation to the king, which, in the name of the Marranos, offered him and the pope a considerable sum of money, on condition that the work of persecution and confiscation should be abandoned. But Ferdinand persisted in his determination, and the Inquisition continued its work with redoubled zeal.

In their despair the Marranos resorted to extreme measures. They determined to assassinate one of the inquisitors. A plan of action was formed in the house of Luis de Santangel, which still stands in the Mercado of Saragossa. The conspirators were Sancho de Paternoy, chief treasurer of Aragon, who had his own seat in the synagogue of Saragossa ; Alfonso de la Caballeria, vice-chancellor of Aragon ; Juan Pedro Sanchez, brother of Gabriel and Francisco Sanchez ; Pedro de Almazan, Pedro Monfort, Juan de la Abadia, Mateo Ram, Garcia de Moros, Pedro de Vera, and other fellow-sufferers of Saragossa, Calatayud, and Barbastro. The plot was executed at the appointed time ; on the night of September 15, 1485, Pedro Arbués was mortally wounded in the cathedral of La Seo, in Saragossa, by Juan de Esperandeu and Vidal Durango, the latter a Frenchman employed as a tanner by Esperandeu. Two days later Arbués died.* When the queen, who happened at that time to be in Cordova, heard of the murder of the inquisitor, she ordered that stringent proceedings should be instituted without mercy against all Marranos, not merely in Saragossa, but in every city of the land, and that their immense possessions should be confiscated by the state.†

Terrible punishment was inflicted on the conspirators. Juan de Esperandeu, a rich tanner, who owned many houses in the Calle del Coso (where the old Jewish bath for women still exists), was obliged to look on while his father, the tanner Salvador de Esperandeu, was burned at the stake. Juan himself, after his hands had been cut off, was dragged to the market-place on June 30, 1486, together with Vidal Durango, and quartered and burned. Juan de la Abadia, who had attempted suicide in prison, was drawn, quartered, and consigned to the flames. Mateo Ram's hands were chopped off, and he, too, died at the stake. Three months later the sisters of Juan de la Abadia, the knight Pedro Muñoz, and Pedro Monfort, vicar-general of the archbishopric of Saragossa, were

---

* Henry C. Lea, *The Martyrdom of S. Pedro Arbués* [*Papers of the American Hist. Assoc.,* vol. iii. New York, 1889.] The real murderer was Vidal, as is evident from a manuscript receipt preserved in the archives of the Cathedral of Saragossa.

† Pulgar, *Reyes Católicos* [Saragossa, 1567], fol. 184a.

burned as adherents of Judaism. Pedro's brother Jaime Monfort, deputy-treasurer of Catalonia, and his wife were burned in effigy in Barcelona.* The sentence of the chief treasurer, Sancho de Paternoy, was commuted to life imprisonment, at the request of his relative Gabriel Sanchez. In March and August, 1487, the notary Garcia de Moros, Juan Ram, son-in-law of Juan Pedro Sanchez, Juan de Santangel, and the knight Luis de Santangel died in the flames. The banker Juan Pedro Sanchez, the real head of the conspiracy, who had succeeded in escaping to Toulouse, was there recognized by the Aragonese students and arrested, but again secured his freedom. Gaspar de Santa Cruz, who had fled with him from Spain, died in Toulouse. Both were burned in effigy in Saragossa, also the other members of the Sanchez family—the merchant Bernard Sanchez, Brianda his wife, and Alfonso Sanchez, a man of letters ; likewise the merchant Anton Perez, and Garcia Lopez. The wife of Lopez remained in Spain and died at the stake.†

The Inquisition spread terror and alarm every-

---

* *Coleccion de Documentos inéditos del Arch. General de la Corona de Aragon,* xxviii. 146.

† *Libro Verde de Aragon,* in Biblioteca Colombina, fol. 78 sq. ; partly printed in *Revista de España,* xviii. 547-578; and in Amador de los Rios, *Historia de los Judíos,* iii. 616 sq. See also *Revue des Études Juives,* xi. 84 sq.

where. Thousands of Marranos suffered martyrdom for their religion. The more dreadfully they
were persecuted, the greater became their love for
their ancestral faith. Dalman de Tolosa openly
declared that he, his mother, his brothers Gabriel
and Luis, and their wives had, despite all hin-
drances, observed the Jewish law. A member of
this family lived in Naples at the beginning of the
sixteenth century, and was known as the *famoso
mercador Catalan.* The wealthy Jacob of Casafranca, who had been deputy-treasurer of Catalonia, and whose mother died as a Jewess in the
prison of the Inquisition, frankly confessed that
the rabbi of Gerona had provided him with meat
and all that he needed for the celebration of the
Jewish holidays, and that in his house, in the Plaça
de Trinidad of Barcelona, he had lived in accord-
ance with the precepts of the Jewish religion and
had read the law of Moses. The councillors of
the Inquisition declared all his posterity to be
Judaizers.*

Among those who were led to the great *auto-
de-fe* at Tarragona, on July 18, 1489, clothed in the
garb of penitents, were Andreas Colom, his wife

---

* " Jacobo de Casafranca, loctinent de thesover per lo Rey nos-
tre Senyor en la Principat de Catalunya, habitador de la Ciutat de
Barcelona, de linatge de Jueus," etc. *Coleccion de Documentos
inéditos . . . de Aragon,* xxviii. 171, 188 sq.

Blancha, and his mother-in-law Francisca Colom. They all confessed that they had observed the rites, ceremonies, and holidays of the Jews.* What must have been the feelings of Christopher Columbus, or Colón,† when he heard that members of the Jewish race bore his name, and had been condemned by the Inquisition?

---

* " Nosaltres Andreu Colom franci Vilagut . . . tots del Archabisbat de Tarragona de nostra libera franquea agradable e spontanea voluntat abjuram renuntiam apartam e eunyam de nosaltret tota e en special aquesta de que som intamats e testificats la qual nosaltres havem confessada ço es de guardar e observar les ceremonies de la Ley de Moyses e fer los ritus e ceremonies e les solemnitats dels jueus les quals en special quiscu de nosaltres ha confessades les quals mes largament son contengendes en la sentencia que contra nosaltres ses donada e declarada." *Coleccion de Documentos inéditos . . . de Aragon,* xxviii. 37 sq.

† He was also called Colom. Winsor, *Columbus,* 157.

CHAPTER IV.

THE ambitious plan which Ferdinand and Isabella energetically strove to realize was to establish a great kingdom, strengthened by political and religious unity. They desired, above all, to bring to an end the dominion of the Moors in Spain, and to expel the Mohammedans from the Peninsula.

When Columbus came to Spain, the war with the Moors had already begun. The systematic confiscation of the property of the "secret" Jews who had been condemned by the Inquisition brought enormous sums of money into the state treasury, and furnished Ferdinand and Isabella with means to continue the war. The victorious Spanish troops had already pressed forward and captured Zahara, Ronda, which had long been called "the Jew's town" (*de los Judios*), Setenil, and several other fortified cities.

It was after the close of the campaign of 1485 that the king and queen were first informed of

Columbus's presence in Spain, and of his project. They received this information from Luis de la Cerda, the brave Duke of Medina-Celi. Toward the close of that year he wrote from Rota to Isabella that he was sheltering in his palace a Genoese named Cristóbal Colón, who had come from Portugal, and who asserted that he could undoubtedly find a new ocean-route to India. The duke also wrote that he would gladly have placed the required ships at Columbus's disposal for the proposed voyage, and would have fitted out the expedition at his own expense, if it were not contrary to the law of the land, and contrary to the will of the queen. The duke was requested to induce the foreign projector to present himself before her.*

With letters of introduction from the duke to the queen and to Alonso de Quintanilla, the chief supervisor of the finances of Castile, Columbus proceeded to Cordova in January, 1486, and here, in May, he was accorded an audience with the Spanish rulers. In order to gain the favor of the pious queen, he wrapped himself in the mantle of

---

* The letter of the duke to the queen, and her answer, as well as the letter which Ferdinand and Isabella ordered Quintanilla to write to the duke, are no longer extant ; they are known to us through the communication sent by the duke to Cardinal Mendoza, March 19, 1493.

religious fanaticism. He asserted that his undertaking was mainly in the interest of the Church ;
that he desired to disseminate Christianity in the
newly discovered lands ; and that, with the gold
found in the ancient and much-renowned Ophir,
the Holy Sepulchre could be wrested from the in-
fidels. The confiding and fanatic Isabella listened
to him with enthusiasm, and her soul was filled
with joy in anticipation of making converts to
Christianity. The king was actuated by wholly
different motives. He had in mind the acquisition
of territory rather than the dissemination of religion. He also took into account the cost of the
enterprise and the dangers of failure, as well as
the possible advantages. By nature distrustful,
calculating, and suspicious, he was very reserved
towards Columbus, who, in his shabby dress, had
given the king the impression that he was an
adventurer. Ferdinand thought that he must
be all the more cautious because the Genoese
had been repelled by the King of Portugal, the
ruler of a state renowned above all for its maritime discoveries. Ferdinand and Isabella soon
agreed that it was not an opportune time to accept
the proposition made by Columbus. Like the
King of Portugal, they determined to refer the
plan for consideration to a learned commission.
They named as its president the Prior of Prado,

the noble Hernando de Talavera, who as confessor of the queen enjoyed her full confidence, and who, as archbishop of Granada, was afterwards so outrageously persecuted by the Inquisition. This commission, which consisted of cosmographers and other eminent scholars, held several sittings, and to it Columbus submitted an exact plan of his enterprise, which he explained and interpreted. But either he failed to be explicit or the commissioners did not wish to understand him, for they reached the same conclusions as the Junta of Lisbon three years before ; namely, that Columbus's assertions could not possibly be true, and that there were no unknown lands to be discovered. They strongly advised the king and queen not to venture into so vague an enterprise, for it would result in no advantage, but only in a loss of money and prestige.* Ferdinand, who in the midst of war could not find time carefully to examine Columbus's arguments, managed to induce the queen to put off the navigator with friendly words. Columbus was informed that while the war was pending such an important matter could not be settled, but that it should be considered as soon as peace was established.† This amounted to a rejection of the project. Columbus was

---

* Las Casas, *Historia de las Indias,* cap. 29.
† *Ibid.*, cap. 29 ; *Vida del Almirante,* cap. II.

obliged, moreover, to endure the hatred and pungent derision of the courtiers and of all those who had heard of his plans. They all regarded him as a scheming adventurer, and in Cordova they derisively called him "The man with the cloak full of holes."

The unfavorable answer of Ferdinand and Isabella was a crushing blow not merely to Columbus, but also to his friends and patrons—to Alonso de Quintanilla, who had compassionately sheltered him for some time under his roof, and especially to Diego de Deza, a learned theologian of Jewish descent, whom Columbus himself reckons among his most influential patrons and supporters. Diego de Deza had a good reputation and was much esteemed. He had charge of the education of the heir-apparent, Prince Don Juan, and he was Bishop of Salamanca, as well as professor of theology at the university of that city, at that time the most celebrated seat of learning in the whole world. To diminish the force of the Junta's verdict he desired to refer Columbus's plan of discovery to eminent cosmographers and mathematicians for further examination. This he actually did without delay. He caused Columbus to come to Salamanca, and summoned to a conference the most distinguished professors of the university—mathematicians, astrologers, and cosmographers.

At its sessions, which were held at Valcuevo, near Salamanca, Columbus presented and defended his project.[*] Among others, there participated in this conference the astrologer Fray Antonio de Marchena, who always championed Columbus's cause, and the Jewish astrologer Abraham Zacuto, who, by his important contributions to his branch of knowledge, materially promoted Columbus's undertaking.

Abraham Zacuto, or Çacuto, was born in Salamanca about the year 1440, and was commonly called Zacuto of Salamanca.[†] His ancestors came from South France, and, as he himself informs us in his celebrated chronicle,[‡] they remained steadfastly loyal to their religion in spite of all persecutions. He devoted himself to the study of mathematics, and especially astronomy, and won the favor of the Bishop of Salamanca, who allowed

---

* "El Illmo Sr. D. Fr. Diego de Deza, que fue obispo de esta ciudad . . . dio parto á los matematicos de esta celebre universidad. Hizoles juntas y retrados á la casa de estos PP. que tienen dos leguas de esta ciudad, llamado Valcuevo." Dorado, *Historia de la Ciudad de Salamanca* [Salamanca, 1776], 225.

Columbus was at Salamanca "á comunicar sus razones con los maestros de Astrologia y Cosmografia que leian estas facultades en la Universidad." Ant. Remesal, *Historia de Chiapa,* lib. 2, cap. 7. Concerning the Junta of Salamanca, see Tomas Rodriguez Pinilla, *Colon en España, Estud. hist. crít.* [Madrid, 1884].

† *Jochasin* (ed. Filipowski), 57ª.

‡ *Ibid.,* 223ª.

him to attend the university of that city. Here he became professor of astronomy,* and many Christian and Mohammedan disciples revered him as their teacher. His chief astronomical work was the *Almanach Perpetuum* with tables of the sun, moon, and stars, which, as his pupil Augustin Ricci informs us,† was prepared between 1473 and 1478, at the request of his patron, the bishop, to whom it was dedicated. It was translated from Hebrew into Latin and Spanish by his pupil Joseph Vecinho, or Vizino, and was printed at the press of Magister Samuel d'Ortas in Leiria. Owing to its wide circulation‡ it went through several editions during the author's lifetime.§

---

* The following is an extract from the dedication to the Bishop of Salamanca, prefixed to the *Almanach :* "Salmantini collegū alumnū me quantūcūque adesse voluisti, docturum videlicet quadruuiales facultates." Jachia confuses Saragossa with Salamanca when he asserts (*Schalschelet*, 50ᵃ) that Zacuto was also professor at Saragossa.

† "Abraham Zacuth, quem præceptorem in Astronomia habuimus in ciuitate Salamancha, jussu Episcopi tabulas astronomicas composuit." Ricci, *De motu octaviæ sphæræ* [Paris, 1521], p. 4.

‡ On page 222ᵃ of his *Jochasin,* written in 1505, Zacuto rightly says : "My Tables are used in all Spain and also in the Orient."

§ This exceedingly rare book, which was first printed at Leiria in 1496, is entitled *Almanach perpetuum cuyas Radix est annum 1473 compositum ab excell. magistro in astronomia nomine bocrat Zacutus.* As far as I am aware, Abraham Zacuto is here for the first time called Bocrat. Was Abraham Bocrat of

Columbus fully acknowledged the importance of Zacuto's contributions to science. He valued particularly Zacuto's *Almanach* and his *Tables*, with the improved quadrennial reckoning, the use of which was much simpler than anything hitherto known, including even the *Ephemerides* of the German astronomer Johannes Müller, commonly called Regiomontanus. Zacuto's *Tables* always accompanied Columbus on his voyages, and rendered him

---

whom Abraham Gavison sings Abraham Zacuto? The work ends thus : " Expliciunt table tablarum astrorum Raby Abraham Zacuti astronome ser. regis emanuel Rex portugaliæ et cet. cum canonibus traductis a lingua ebrayca in latinum per magistrum Joseph vizinum discipulum ejus actoris." Then comes the title : "Tabule Tabularum celestium motuum astronomi Zacuti necnon stelarum fixarum longitudinem ac latitudinem ad motus vnitatem mira diligentia reducte ac in principio canones ordinatissime incipiunt felici sidere." Two tables follow. The next fifteen pages contain the *Canones en Romance* with the final words: " Aqui se acaba la recela de las tablas tresladadas del abrayco en latin e de latin en noestro vulgar romance por mestre jusepe vezino decipulo del actor de las tablas."

Columbus's copy of the work, with notes and glosses in his handwriting, is in the Colombina. See *Bibl. Colombina con notas bibl. del Dr. D. Simón de la Rosa y López* [Seville, 1888], i. 3.

The *Almanach Perpetuum*, "Joseph vecino traductor," was published in Venice, July 15, 1502, 4to. The *Tables*, revised by Alfonso de Corduba, appeared in Venice in 1496 and 1512, 4to, under the title *Tabulæ motuum cælestium cum additamentis Alphonsis Hispani de Corduba.* There is a MS. Hebrew translation of the *Almanach* in the royal library at Munich. See M. Steinschneider, *Cat. Cod. MSS. Bibl. Reg. Monacensis* [Munich, 1875], p. 49.

inestimable service. To them, in fact, he and his crew once owed their lives. On his last voyage he had visited the coast of Veragua, the name of which is still perpetuated in the title of his present descendant, the Duke of Veragua. In its rich mines he found plenty of gold and precious stones. After leaving Veragua a terrible hurricane greatly injured his only two surviving caravels, rendering them unseaworthy. After he reached Jamaica he was in a desperate plight. The ungrateful Francisco de Porras had stirred up a conspiracy against him ; Columbus himself was prostrated by illness ; the natives were hostile to him and threatened his life ; the few sailors who remained loyal to him were disheartened, and exhausted by hunger. The admiral and his followers anticipated certain death.

Thereupon he resorted to an expedient which is characteristic of him and of his time. By means of Zacuto's *Tables* he ascertained that there would be an eclipse of the moon on February 29, 1504. He then summoned certain caciques, or native chiefs, and told them that the God of the Spaniards was very angry with them because they did not give him and his sailors sufficient food, and that God would punish them by depriving them of the light of the moon, and by mercilessly subjecting them to the most pernicious influences. When night arrived, and the moon was invisible, the caciques and their followers raised a doleful wail, and, throwing themselves at the admiral's feet, they promised to provide him with plenty of provisions, and implored him to avert from them the impending evil. Columbus then retired on the pretense of communing with the Deity. When the thick darkness began to vanish, and the moon began to appear, he again came forth, and announced to the expectant caciques that their contrition had appeased the divine wrath. The full light of the moon soon beamed forth, and Columbus's object was attained ; he encountered no more hostility, and obtained an abundance of food. "Thursday, February 29, 1504," says Columbus, " as I was in the Indies, on the island of Jamaica, in the harbor of Sancta Gloria, situated about in the middle of the northern side of the island, there was an eclipse of the moon. As it began before the sun went down, I could note its termination only; the full light of the moon became visible exactly two and a half hours after nightfall. The difference in time between the Island of Jamaica in the Indies and the Island of Calis in Spain is seven hours and fifteen minutes, so that the sun sets in Calis seven hours and fifteen minutes earlier than in Jamaica." Columbus then refers to Zacuto's *Almanach*, the statement of which regarding the moon's eclipse exactly agrees with Columbus's observation.*

There can be no doubt that Zacuto, who made the personal acquaintance of Columbus in Salamanca, called the latter's attention to his treatises,† and that he also orally communicated to Columbus his theory concerning storms in the equinoctial regions—a theory which was of value to navigators. Zacuto, like his protector, Diego de Deza, was one of those who declared in favor of Columbus and his undertaking, and asserted that "the distant Indies, separated from us by great seas and vast tracts of land, can be reached, though the enterprise is hazardous."‡

The conference of Salamanca, in which Colum-

---

* "Jueves 29 de Febrero de 1504 estando yo en las yndias en la ysla de Janahica en el poerto que se diz de Sancta Gloria que es casi en el medio de la ysla, de la parte septentrional, obo eclipsis de la luna, y porque el comienco fue primero que el sol se pusiese non pude nótar saluo el termino de quando la luna acabo de volver en su claridad, y esto fue muy certificado dos oras y media pasadas de la noche. Cinco compolletas muy ciertas. La diferencia del medio de la ysla de Janahica en las yndias con la ysla de Calis en españa es siete oras y quinze minutos, de manera que en Calis se puso el sol primero que en Janahica con siete oras y quinze minutos de ora, vide Almanach." *Libro de las Profecias,* 59 sq.

† See above, p. 14.

‡ Gaspar Correa, *Lendas da India,* in *Collecção de Monumentos ineditos para a historia das Conquistas dos Portuguezes* [Lisbon, 1858], i. 10.

bus's resolute demeanor won the admiration of many and the sympathy of all, determined his fate, though its action was not of an official character, like that of the Junta of Cordova. The representations made by Diego de Deza and other learned men induced Ferdinand and Isabella to take Columbus into their service, and on May 5, 1487, they ordered the royal treasurer to deliver three thousand maravedis to the poor Genoese. Toward the end of August another sum of four thousand maravedis was assigned to him, with the express command to proceed to Malaga, which had been captured by the Spanish army a few weeks before. Here he became acquainted with the two most distinguished Jews of Spain, who were then at the king's court—the chief farmer of the taxes, Abraham Senior, of whom we have already spoken, and his friend Isaac Abravanel. They had undertaken to provision the royal armies, and by making great sacrifices they had done this to the special satisfaction of Queen Isabella. They were of extraordinary service to the kingdom, for they not merely devoted their own enormous fortunes to the purchase of arms and provisions, but they also induced other rich Jews to follow their example.*

---

* Amador de los Rios, *Historia de los Judíos de España y Portugal,* iii. 296 sq.

Don Isaac Abravanel belonged to an old and distinguished family. His grandfather, the "great" Samuel Abravanel, the richest and most influential Jew in Valencia, temporarily changed his religion in consequence of the great persecution of 1391, and called himself Alfonso Fernandez de Vilanova, after the name of one of his estates.* Samuel's son Judah Abravanel settled in Lisbon, and became treasurer of Prince Ferdinand, who, before his campaign against the Moors of Tangiers, made provision for the prompt payment of more than half a million reis which he had borrowed from Don Judah. Isaac Abravanel enjoyed the complete confidence of King Affonso V. of Portugal, and was on the most friendly terms with the members of the house of Braganza. But after Affonso's death he was obliged to resort to flight, as he was a friend of the powerful Duke of Braganza, whom King João II. had condemned to death. He went to Castile and soon won the favor of the king and queen.† It is possible that

---

* " E hir lo gran don Samuel Abravalla se batejá ab gran solemnitat en lo real d'En Gastó, sots padrinatge del marqués, é ha nom Alfonso Fernandez de Vilanova, per un loch, que éll ha en lo marquesat, apelat Vilanova." *Carta de los Jurados de Valencia,* in Amador de los Rios, *Historia X de los Judío,* ii. 603. According to Zacuto (*Jochasin,* 224) he called himself Juan de Sevilla.

† Concerning Isaac Abravanel's life and works, see Kayserling, *Geschichte der Juden in Portugal,* 72. sq.

Columbus, during his residence in the capital of Portugal, had already made the acquaintance of this honored and accomplished man. Isaac Abravanel was one of the first to render financial assistance to Columbus's undertaking.

CHAPTER V.

WE do not know why Columbus was called to
Malaga or how long he stayed there. He soon
returned to Cordova, where he became intimate
with Beatrice Enriquez, a poor girl, who has been
erroneously called the daughter of a Jew. He
was soon neglected again by the king and queen,
who gradually ceased to grant him subsidies. He
lived in the greatest poverty with his mistress
Beatrice, by whom he had a son. Tired of pro-
longed delays, he resumed the negotiations with
the King of Portugal which had been discontinued
several years before ; but these new overtures
were also unsuccessful, and he now determined
to lay his project before the King of France.

He first proceeded to the monastery of La
Rábida near Palos, either to see his son Diego
before leaving Spain, or, more probably, to inform
his patron, the Prior Juan Perez de Marchena, of

his plans and to bid him farewell. At the gate of this monastery, which was situated on an eminence, he had knocked as a poor pilgrim on his arrival in Spain, and had begged for bread and water for his little son. The prior, who was considerably interested in Columbus's plans, did all in his power to prevent the proposed departure from Spain, and he was seconded in his efforts by Garcia Fernandez, the physician of Palos.* Marchena, who had been the queen's confessor, and was highly esteemed by her as a good astrologer, wrote an urgent letter to Isabella, recommending the Genoese and his undertaking in the warmest terms. This letter was carried to the queen, who was then at Santa Fé, by Sebastian Rodriguez, a mariner of Lepe. The neighboring city of Granada had already been forced to capitulate. In this splendid Moorish town a revolt had just broken out among the Moslems, but they had been somewhat pacified by Ferdinand's promise that all Moors and Jews should enjoy religious freedom, and that they might depart without hindrance.†

---

* Dr. Calatraveño, *Hechos médicos relacionados con el descubrimiento de América* [Madrid, 1892].

† The original manuscript of the capitulation of Granada (in the Escurial, MS. 7 del siglo xv.) has the following : "Otrosi suplicamos a vuestras Altezas manden dar sus cartas de seguro

After deliberating with the king, Isabella wrote at once to the prior that he should come as soon as possible to the royal camp, and bring with him Columbus, who was still in the monastery, awaiting an answer. She also sent two thousand maravedis in order that the navigator might appear before their majesties decently clothed. In company with the prior he then started for Santa Fé, and arrived there, in the midst of the tumult of war, in December, 1491, shortly before the crescent disappeared from the western tower of the Alhambra. In Santa Fé he found his most influential patron, Pedro Gonzales de Mendoza, the primate, or, as he is called by Peter Martyr,* "the third king of Spain," who presided over a meeting of distinguished men summoned to examine the project of discovery. Columbus boldly advocated his scheme, and soon convinced the primate that his assertions were true. It was not difficult for the latter to induce the queen to give her approval to the plan of exploration.

After a seven years' conflict, comparable only with the Trojan war, Granada fell into the power

---

para los Judios, y licencia para levar lo suyo, e que si sin culpa de alguno por no haber navio alguno quedaren en la costa que haya termino para se partir." In the margin are the words : " Que se haya."

* Pedro Martyr, *Epistolæ*, lib. 8, epist. 159.

of Spain. On Friday, January 2, 1492, the Spanish standard first floated from the highest tower of the old Moorish palace, and the two sovereigns ceremoniously entered the conquered Moorish capital. On the same day Ferdinand announced to all the cities of his kingdom that, after many great conflicts which had cost much noble blood, it had pleased God to allow the Christian armies to vanquish the Moors. Since the conquest of Granada papal gratitude has permitted the ruler of Spain to bear the title His Most Catholic Majesty.

In all the cities of Spain the fall of the Moorish dominion and the triumph of the Christian religion were celebrated with songs of rejoicing. The Jews went about in sorrow and with bowed heads, for the conquest of the Moslem also decided their fate, in spite of the important part which they had played in securing the victory; from the palace of the Alhambra the Catholic king and queen soon issued the cruel edict of their expulsion. At the pompous spectacle of the entry of the Christian armies into Granada there were present two men of extraordinary importance, two wholly dissimilar men, with whose acts Spain's later greatness as well as her downfall, her whole distracted destiny, was closely connected—a proud priest and a morose beggar.

The priest was Cardinal Ximenez de los Cisneros, the very learned grand inquisitor, who wished to turn all Moors and Jews into Christians, and who persecuted the Marranos with the utmost rigor. The beggar was Christopher Columbus, with whom the two sovereigns now began to negotiate in earnest. Within reach of the object of his long-cherished hopes and desires, Columbus was impelled by his ambition and insatiable avarice to make enormous demands ; he wished to be appointed admiral, viceroy, and governor for life over all lands which he might discover. Ferdinand was not inclined to grant such demands or to concede such far-reaching privileges. Hence the negotiations with Columbus were suspended, and in January, 1492, he left Granada with the definite purpose of going to the French court.

Then, when his cause seemed to be lost, several persons resolutely interposed in his favor ; they were Juan Cabrero, Luis de Santangel, Gabriel Sanchez, and Alfonso de la Caballeria, all men of Jewish extraction. When Luis de Santangel heard that the negotiations with Columbus had been definitely broken off, he felt as much sorrow and distress as if he himself had been afflicted with some great misfortune.[*]

Let us pause to inquire who Luis de Santangel

---

[*] Las Casas, *Historia de las Indias,* cap. 32.

was. In the fifteenth and sixteenth centuries the
family of Santangel or Sancto Angelo was one of
the richest, most influential, and most powerful in
Aragon. When, in consequence of great persecutions and of the Jew-baiting sermons of Vicente
Ferrer, many Jews in Calatayud, Daroca, Fraga,
Barbastro, and other cities changed their religion in order to save their lives, the Santangels
also adopted Christianity. Like the Villanuevas,
whose ancestor was Moses Patagon,* and the
Clementes, who were descended from Moses
Chamorro, the Santangels also emanated from
Calatayud, the ancient Calat-al-yehud, which in the
fourteenth century had one of the richest Jewish
communities in Aragon. The ancestor of the Santangels is said to have been the learned Azarias
Ginillo, whose wife could not be induced to for-
sake Judaism, even outwardly. A few years later,
however, she married Bonafos de la Caballeria,
and, together with her husband, she followed the
example of Azarias and became a Christian.
Azarias Ginillo, or Luis de Santangel, as he
called himself, was an eminent jurist. He had
several sons and daughters. One of these, together

---

* Also called Pazagon. Members of this family also resided
in Portugal. Isaac Pazagon was president of the Jewish community in Coimbra about the year 1360. See Kayserling, *Geschichte der Juden in Portugal*, 24.

with her lover, a certain Marzilla, was murdered by her husband. The other daughter married Pedro Gurrea, a secret Jew, and their son Gaspar wedded Anna de la Caballeria, a secret Jewess.[*] Azarias's sons, Alfonso—who, like his father, studied law—Juan Martin, and Pedro Martin, lived in Daroca, and secured protection and privileges from King Ferdinand I. of Aragon.[†]

Azarias-Luis de Santangel was not only learned, but also prosperous, though not wealthy. In the year 1459 his grandsons, the jurist Luis de Santangel, junior, and Leonardo de Santangel of Calatayud, petitioned King Juan of Aragon to allow them to dig for gold and silver coins and other treasures which had been buried by their parents and grandparents. They proposed to dig beneath the houses which, as orphans of tender age, they had inherited from their parents, but which they had afterwards sold to the Jew Abraham Patagon or to his brother Raymundo Lopez. The property adjoined the estates of Fernando Lupo and Luis Sanchez in the Villanueva quarter of Calatayud. Luis de Santangel offered to give to the state treasury one-fifth of all that he might find. The king granted their petition on October 24, 1459, on condition that they should undertake the excava-

---

[*] *Revista de España,* xviii. 249 sq.   [†] Appendix i.

tions at their own expense, and with the consent of Abraham Patagon, the present owner of the houses, and that these houses should be restored to the condition in which they were found.*

In consequence of their keen intellects, their activity, and their wealth, the Santangels secured great influence and high positions of trust ; they were prominent jurists and teachers of law, and occupied important posts in the cortes, in the municipalities, in the administration of the state, and in the Church.

Azarias-Luis de Santangel, who had the reputation of being an excellent lawyer,† attained the position of Zalmedina, or Zavalmedina, a name given to the judge in ordinary of the capital, who was appointed by the king.‡ To escape persecution and to demonstrate his Christian faith, he devoted his son Pedro Martin to the ministry, and the latter became Bishop of Mallorca as well as adviser of King Juan II. Pedro Martin left a legacy to provide for the marriage of poor orphan girls of his family, and by the terms of his will the trust was to be administered by the city of

---

* Appendix ii.

† Zurita, *Anales de la Corona de Aragon,* vol. iv., lib. 16, cap. 25.

‡ Zalmedina is an abbreviation of Zavalmedina, which is derived from an Arabic word meaning "lord," and from *medina,* "city." *Coleccion de Documentos inéditos de Aragon,* viii. 115.

Barbastro.* Another Martin de Santangel, the
bishop's nephew, became provincial of Aragon,
and resided in Saragossa. Another Luis de
Santangel, acting as ambassador of King Alfonso
V. of Aragon, negotiated with the Sultan of
Babylonia concerning a commercial treaty. The
most far-reaching influence was attained by those
members of the family who had houses and property in Daroca, Barbastro, Teruel, Alcañiz, and in
other towns of Aragon and Valencia, especially
in Calatayud, Valencia, and Saragossa.

The lawyer Luis de Santangel, the one who had
sought for the treasures buried by his parents in
Calatayud, held the high office of treasury advo-
cate (*fisci advocatus*). The names of Luis de
Santangel and Luis de la Caballeria, the treasurer-
general, were subscribed to a patent of nobility
and grant of privileges issued on December 4,
1461, in Calatayud, by King Juan of Aragon, to
his "well-beloved" soldier Juan Gilbert and his
descendants.† At a meeting of the cortes of

---

* " Concordia entre la ciudad de Barbastro y Pedro Lunel y su
Muger D. Maria de Santangel sobre el legado de Pedro de Santangel para casar pupilas . . . . Es patrona de este legado la
ciudad segun la clausula que se incerta en el testamento del dicho
Pedro de Santangel. Llama descendientes pobres de su linaje y
el legado de 513 livres." (1473.) *Archivo de Zaragoza.*

† The original document, which was formerly in the archives
of Calatayud, is now in the state archives at Alcalá de Henares.

Aragon in the year 1473, this Luis de Santangel represented the knights and nobles, while in the same year Antonio de Santangel of Calatayud represented that city.* The latter interposed on behalf of the Jewish community of Hijar a few days after the expulsion of the Jews from Spain.†
In the middle of the fifteenth century the Santangels of Valencia and Saragossa were the Rothschilds of their time. At the head of the Valencian house was the merchant Luis de Santangel the elder. In the year 1450 Luis already gained the favor of King Alfonso V. of Aragon ; ‡ he also had uninterrupted intercourse with King Juan II. He was farmer of the *de la Mata* salt-works near Valencia, for which, according to a contract of July 9, 1472, he had to pay a yearly rent of 21,100 sueldos to the Marrano Juan de Ribasaltas ; §

---

* Miguel Mir, *Influencia de los Aragoneses en el descubrimiento de América* [Palma de Mallorca, 1892], pp. 29 sq. ; Eduardo Ibarra y Rodríguez, D. *Fernando el Católico y el descubrimiento de América* [Madrid, 1892], pp. 191 sq.

† "Anton de Santangel, habitante en Calatayud, reclama una cuenta sobre la aljama de Judios en Hijar." Borja, Aug. 10, 1492. *Arch. de la Corona de Aragon,* Reg. 3650, fol. 109.

‡ Documents dated Perpignan, March 18 and July 8, 1450. *Arch. de la Corona de Aragon,* Reg. 3253, fol. 132, and Reg. 3254, fol. 58 sq.

§ " . . . valeamus arrendare et titulo arrendamenti concedere vobis delecto et fideli nostro Ludouico de Santoangelo mercatori ciuitatis Valentie natu majori salinas vulgo dictas de

he was also farmer of the royal domains and customs.* After the death of Luis the elder in 1476, his wife Brianda† assumed the management of his business, and his son Luis de Santangel the younger, who was a royal councillor in Valencia, became farmer of the royal domains,‡ while the farming of the salt-works, after the termination of the elder Luis's contract, passed to his relative and partner Jaime de Santangel.§ Jaime's coffers

la mata per set anys," etc. Document dated Ajatero, July 9, 1472. *Arch. de la Corona de Aragon,* Reg. 3641, fol. 26. Beatrice de Ribasaltas, wife of Juan de la Caballeria, was subjected to public penance on July 17, 1491.

* "Orden al mercador de Valencia Luis de Santangel mayor de edad para que de lo que ha de dar al Rey por varon del ordenamiento de peage y otros seruicios pague á Jaime de Santangel criado y copero del Rey 1183 sueldos y seis dineros moned. barcel." Document dated Barcelona, December 28, 1473. *Arch. de la Corona de Aragon,* Reg. 3641, fol. 35.

"Confirmacion del nombramiento de recepcion en las rentas reales de Valencia que á favor de Luis de Santangel mercador en dicha ciudad hizo D. Juan en Barcelona, 16 Agosto, 1475." Burgos, September 9, 1475. There is a confirmation dated Caceres, May 26, 1478. *Arch. de la Corona de Aragon,* Reg. 3519, fol. 38, and Reg. 3633, fol. 91.

† "Causam vertentem propter Briandam de Sanctangel viduam Ludouici et Jacobum de Sanctangel eorumque filios tam ut heredes patris eorum." *Ibid.,* Reg. 3633, fol. 9.

‡ The contract is dated Madrigal, April 8, 1476. *Ibid.,* Reg. 3633, fol. 18. See also Reg. 3547, fol. 127 sq. : "Luis de Sanctangel consejero ciudadano de Valencia."

§ "Concordia entre el Rey y el magnífico Jaime de Santangel escribano de racion y consejero de Su Majestad sobre las salinas

were always open to Juan II., who appointed him royal cup-bearer, and they were also open to Ferdinand, his son and successor. Jaime lent the latter large sums of money to subdue the rebellious Catalonians, to recover the county of Rousillon from the King of France, to whom it had been pledged, and to conquer Granada.* Whenever Ferdinand needed money he appealed to his friends the Santangels in Valencia, and never in vain.

To this family which stood in such high repute in all Aragon, Catalonia, and Valencia, the Inquisition proved fatal. As we have already seen, the introduction of the Holy Office was opposed by the richest and most distinguished Marranos of Saragossa. The Santangels were among those who, at heart true to their old faith, headed the conspiracy against the Inquisitor Pedro d'Arbués. As the spot where Arbués received his death-blow

---

de la mata de Valencia." Victoria, December 29, 1484. *Arch. de la Corona de Aragon*, Reg. 3641, fol. 2.

* "El Rey conceso á su copero Jacobo de Sanctangelo treze mil sueldos de moneda barcel. en pago de los consilios que al monarca habia prestado en la guerra para reclamar á la obediencia al Principal de Cataluña." Barcelona, October 30, 1473. *Ibid.*, Reg. 3461, fol. 44. He aided the king with the same sum "en la reduccion de Rossillon que adhuc sub obediencia regis detinetur." *Ibid.*, Reg. 3519, fol. 173. For the loan "in hoc bello quod contra Granatam gerimus," see the document dated Cordova, September 1, 1485. *Ibid.*, Reg. 3641, fol. 105.

is still pointed out in the metropolitan church of La Seo, so too one may still see in the large and beautiful market-place, or Mercado, of Saragossa the stately houses which in the flourishing days of the Aragonese capital belonged to Luis and Juan de Santangel.* The Santangels were also among the first Jewish heretics to mount the funeral pile. The first victim of the Inquisition in Saragossa was Martin de Santangel, who was burned July 28, 1486; eleven months later, August 18, 1487, Mosen Luis de Santangel, father-in-law of the treasurer Gabriel Sanchez, met the same fate. On July 10, 1489, the mother of Gabriel Gonçalo de Santangel, and six years later Gabriel himself, died at the stake. The lawyer Juan de Santangel and his brother Luis, who both resorted to timely flight and reached Bordeaux in safety, were burned in effigy, the one on March 17, 1487, the other on June 1, 1492 ; all their property, real and personal, was confiscated by the state. Juan was exiled forever from Spain, and his three daughters, Louisa, Agnes and Laura, who had been reared in affluence, were reduced to extreme

---

* In the year 1512 Juan Sanchez de Romeral, "procurador sindico de los Jurados de Zaragoza," grants a licence for the repair of the façade of a house adjoining "con casas de Micer Luis de Santangel, y con casas de los herederos de Juan de Albacer é con el mercado." *Arch. del ayuntamiento de Zaragoza.*

poverty. Even the hard-hearted Ferdinand was moved at this spectacle ; as a special token of royal grace and in recognition of their father's services, he granted them, on January 19, 1488, a yearly pension of 1,500 sueldos out of the taxes of the Jewish community in Jaca.* We do not know whether this annuity came to an end with the expulsion of the Jews and the cessation of their taxes.

Snares were constantly laid by the Holy Office to entrap the members of the Santangel family and to secure their property. Jaime Martin was burned on March 20, 1488; Donosa de Santangel six months later; Simon de Santangel and his wife Clara Lunel, betrayed by their own son, were burned in Lerida on July 30, 1490.† In order to have a quasi-legal pretext for confiscating their property for the use of the state, Violante de Santangel,‡ the wife of Alfonso Gomez of Huesca, and Gabriel de Santangel of Barbastro were condemned, and their remains were exhumed and publicly burned. Gabriel's estates were sold by the king to Miguel Vivo, Abbot of Aljoro, for

---

* See Appendix iii.

† *Revue des Études Juives,* xi. 87.

‡ "Violante de Santangel, muger de Alfonso Gomez en Huesca, condemnata et ejus ossa exhumata et igni tradita, sus bienes á la Curia." Granada, September 20, 1491. *Arch. de la Corona de Aragon,* Reg. 3649, fol. 18.

18,000 sueldos.* All the members of the family
who escaped with their lives were at least pilloried
as Jews or Jewish heretics. Thus the jurist Pedro
de Santangel, Juan Thomas and Miguel de Santangel,† the wife of Lopez-Patagon, and Lucretia
de Santangel, all had to go in public procession
clothed as penitents and solemnly swear never
again to practice Jewish rites. The Inquisition
carried on, in fact, a veritable war of destruction
against all the members of this family ; without
regard to age, sex, or position, they were consigned to the flames or obliged to do public penance, and that, too, even as late as the sixteenth
century.‡

On July 17, 1491, Luis de Santangel also appeared in a variegated *sambenito* as an adherent
of Judaism. He stands in the foreground of the
event of that time which figures so prominently
in the world's annals ; impartial historians must

---

* "Gabriel de Santangel de Barbastro condemnatus et ejus ossa
exhumata et igni tradita, sus bienes á la Curia, y despues el Rey
los venden á D. Miguel Viuo abad de Aljoro á cambio de 18,000
sueldos." Granada, May 12, 1492. *Ibid.*, Reg. 3650, fol. 44.

† Miguel was an alderman of Saragossa.

‡ The following were burned : Isabel de Santangel, October
4, 1495 ; Fernando de Santangel of Barbastro, October 19, 1496 ;
Juana de Santangel, wife of Pedro de Santa Fé, September 13,
1499. A Luis de Santangel of Calatayud did public penance on
June 10, 1493, and another Luis de Santangel on October 19,
1496. See *El Libro Verde, in Revista de España*, vol. xviii.

unhesitatingly assign to him an important rôle in the discovery of America.

He was the son of the rich Luis de Santangel who was the farmer of the royal taxes and customs in Valencia, an office which he himself subsequently held ; he was the nephew of the Luis de Santangel who died at the stake in Saragossa. King Ferdinand appointed him *escribano de racion,* chancellor of the royal household in Aragon. He also held the same influential position of *contador mayor,* or comptroller-general, in Aragon which was occupied by Alonso de Quintanilla in Castile. He was a favorite of King Ferdinand, enjoyed the latter's complete confidence, knew all his secrets, and transacted all kinds of business for him. The king held him in high esteem for his fidelity, his sagacity, his extraordinary industry 380Xand adm talent, his sterling integrity and his complete devotion to the crown ; whenever Ferdinand wrote to him, he called him "the good Aragonese, excellent, well-beloved councillor."* On the other hand, Luis de Santangel owed his royal friend not only his eminent position but also his life ; had it not been for the

---

* " . . . en atencion á sus meritos, fides, solertia, industria, sufficientia, disposicione et animi probitate." *Arch. de la Corona de Aragon,* Reg. 3616, fol. 169 sq., 208, etc. See also Victor Balaguer, *Cristóbal Colón* [Madrid, 1892], p. 43.

king's direct intervention, he and his children would have shared the fate of his uncle and that of many of his relatives.

Luis de Santangel was the Beaconsfield of Spain. Like that English statesman—who was of Jewish stock and whose ancestors were also persecuted by the Inquisition and driven from Spain—Luis was characterised at once by particularism and universalism, enthusiasm and sagacity, subjective patriotism and objective devotion to other nationalities. He was a good Aragonese, and yet he worked for the unity of Spain ; he was ardently devoted to his country, and he carefully considered the advantages which it would derive from maritime discoveries. As the head of a great mercantile house in Valencia and as farmer of the royal customs, he had intercourse with Genoese merchants long before Columbus came to Spain. Already in 1479 he was commissioned by Ferdinand to settle a disputed question in which some Genoese mariners in Valencia were concerned ; the dispute was regarding certain customs-duties. At the same time he was also ordered to pay for the cloth imported from Lombardy for the use of the royal household.*

---

* The document is dated Trugillo, February 6, 1479. *Arch. de la Corona de Aragon,* Reg. 3633, fol. 90 ; see also Reg. 3633, fol. 70.

Probably Columbus was introduced to the merchant of Valencia by some of his countrymen, and may have early made Santangel's acquaintance.

Luis de Santangel became the leader of the Aragonese who at the last moment successfully interposed on behalf of Columbus. He was actively assisted by the royal chamberlain Juan Cabrero, the son of Martin Cabrero and Isabel de Paternoy, who were both of Jewish lineage and whose kinsmen were victims of the Inquisition.* Juan was the confidential friend and constant companion of Ferdinand the Catholic; he fought at the king's side in the Moorish wars, and was his faithful advisor in all affairs of state; he enjoyed Ferdinand's confidence to such an extent that he was made the executor of the king's will.

As soon as Santangel heard of Columbus's departure and the termination of his negotiations, he went to the queen, if not at Ferdinand's request, at least with his consent, and earnestly expressed his surprise that so magnanimous a patron of great enterprises had not the courage to enter on an undertaking from which she could reasonably anticipate enormous wealth, great increase of territory, and immortal glory both for

---

* Juan de Paternoy's remains were burned as those of a Jewish heretic, at the *auto-de-fe* in Saragossa on June 20, 1497.

the crown and for the Church.   He represented
to her that the amount of money demanded for
the enterprise was comparatively small, and that
the remuneration which the explorer demanded
for such discoveries as he might make, should not
occasion much hesitation.   Columbus himself,
Santangel went on to say, undertook to bear a
part of the expense, and ventured his honor, nay
even his life.   In all probability the Genoese was
a wise and sagacious man, well qualified to achieve
success.   Many eminent scholars to whom the
queen had submitted his project for examination
had approved of it, and Columbus's opponents
could advance no valid arguments against his con-
tentions.   If, as Columbus predicted, some other
European power should have the good fortune to
act as his patron and to reap the fruits of these
discoveries, the kingdom of Spain, its rulers, and
the whole nation would suffer much shame and
detriment.   If the queen did not seize this opportunity, she would reproach herself all her life ;
her enemies would deride her, and her descendants would blame her ; she would impair her
honor and the renown of her royal name ; she
would injure her states and the welfare of her
subjects.*

These arguments of Santangel produced a pro-

---

* Las Casas, *Historia de las Indias,* cap. 32.

found impression upon the queen. She thanked him for his advice, and promised him her consent to the undertaking ; but she desired to wait awhile until the kingdom recovered its strength, for its financial resources had been exhausted by the recent, long-continued war. It is said that she even promised to pledge her jewels to secure money for the equipment of the armada, if Columbus could not brook further delay in the execution of his enterprise.* Santangel, the story continues, was much delighted at the queen's resolve, and declared that it was not necessary for her to pledge her jewels ; he would be pleased, he said, to advance the money necessary for the expedition, and would be glad of the opportunity to perform so small a service for her and for his master the king.† This story, invented to glorify Queen Isabella, has recently been relegated to the realm of fable.‡ The sale of crowns and jewels by Spanish rulers was not, however, a rare occurrence.

---

* "Mas prestándole Luis de Santangel diez y seis mil Ducados sobre sus joyas." Pizarro y Orellano, *Varones ilustres del Nuevo Mundo* [Madrid, 1639], p. 10. This assertion is accepted by Prescott in his *History of Ferdinand and Isabella,* and by Washington Irving in his excellent *Life of Columbus.*

† Las Casas, *Historia de las Indias,* cap. 32 ; Muñoz, *Historia del Nuevo Mundo,* vol. ii., cap. 31.

‡ See the excellent essay of the learned academician Cesáreo Fernández Duro, *Las joyas de Isabel la Católica,* in his *Tradiciones infundadas* [Madrid, 1888].

Doña Sancha, wife of Ferdinand I. the Great of Castile, sold her jewels in order to pay the soldiers for their services in the war against the Moors. When Alfonso X. the Wise of Castile, desired to put down the rebellion of the Infante Don Sancho, he borrowed a large sum of money from the Moor Jacob Abd-el-Hacer, and gave him the crown jewels as security. In order to carry on the siege of Algeciras in 1344, Alfonso XI. was compelled to pawn his crown ; and in the expedition against Naples Alfonso V. of Aragon pledged his crown and his table-plate for two hundred and eighty-seven ducats.*

At that time neither Aragon nor Castile, neither Ferdinand nor Isabella, had at their disposal enough money to equip a fleet. Santangel, who was always ready to oblige the crown, advanced seventeen thousand florins—nearly five million maravedis.† The queen's jewels were not de-

---

* P. Fidel Fita, *Boletín de la real Academia de la Historia,* xii. 218.

† " Y porque auia necesidad de dineros para su expedicion, á causa de la guerra, los prestó para fazer la primera armada de las Indias y su descubrimiento el escribano de racion luys de Sant Angel;" Gonçalo Fernandez de Oviedo, *Coronica de las Indias* [1547], p. 5ᵇ. "Hallandose los Reyes en necesidad de dineros para esta empresa, prestó les diez y seys mil Ducados Luys de Sant Angel, su escribano de raciones ;" Garibay, *Compendio historial de las Chronicas de todos los Reynos d'España* [Antwerp, 1571], lib. 19, cap. I, p. 1371. " Y por que los Reyes no tenian

manded as security ; all of them were not, in fact, in her possession at that time, for she had pledged her necklace during the late war. Owing to the jealousy which still exists even at the present day between Castile and Aragon, Aragonese writers* have recently discussed the question whether Luis de Santangel lent this money out of his own pocket or whether he secured it indirectly from the state treasury through Gabriel Sanchez, the treasurer-general of Aragon. Apart from the fact that the treasury of Aragon as well as that of Castile was empty in consequence of the long war with the Moors,† Santangel's extraordinary services in this matter are clearly demonstrated by the excessive praise which Ferdinand accorded his "well-beloved" Luis de Santangel, and by the many proofs of gratitude which the

---

dineros para despacher á Colon, les prestó Luys de Sant Angel, su escribano de racion, seis cuentos de maravedis, que son en cuenta mas gruesa 16,000 ducados;" Gómara, *Historia de las Indias,* cap. 15, p. 167. "Y para el gasto de la Armada prestó Luis de Santangel escribano de raciones de Aragon diez y siete mil florines ;" Bart. Leonarde de Argensola, *Anales,* lib. I, cap. 10.

* Eduardo Ibarra y Rodríguez, D. *Fernando el Católico y el descubrimiento de América* [Madrid, 1892], pp. 164 sq.

† Felipe de la Caballeria of Saragossa had lent 9,022 sueldos to Ferdinand's father, King Juan of Aragon, who died in January, 1479. It was not until 1493 that Gabriel Sanchez was ordered by the king to pay this debt. Document dated Barcelona, August 30, 1493. *Arch. de la Corona de Aragon,* Reg. 3616, fol. 182.

king gave him.* Of these we shall have more
to say later.

That he advanced this money out of his own
pocket is proven beyond question by the original
account-books, which were formerly in the archives
of Simancas and which are still preserved in the
Archivo de Indias in Seville. In the account-book
of Luis de Santangel and the treasurer Francisco
Pinelo, extending from 1491 to 1493, Santangel
is credited with an item of 1,140,000 maravedis
which he gave to the Bishop of Avila† for
Columbus's expedition. In another account-book,
that of Garcia Martinez and Pedro de Monte-
mayor, there is the following item : Alonso de las
Cabezas, treasurer of war in the bishopric of Badajoz, by order of the Archbishop of Granada, dated
May 5, 1492, paid to Alonso de Angulo for Luis
de Santangel, the king's *escribano de racion,* whose
authorization was presented with the aforesaid
order, 2,640,000 maravedis, to wit, 1,500,000 in
payment to Isaac Abravanel of money which he
had lent their majesties in the Moorish war, and
the remaining 1,140,000 maravedis in payment to

---

* See Appendix v. and vi. ; also the document dated Barcelona, May 20, 1493, in *Arch. de la Corona de Aragon,* Reg. 3616,
fol. 169 dorse.

† This Bishop of Avila afterwards became Archbishop of
Granada.

the aforesaid *escribano de racion* of money which he advanced to equip the caravels ordered by their majesties for the expedition to the Indies and to pay Christopher Columbus, the admiral of that fleet.* On May 20, 1493, on which day Ferdinand was particularly occupied with Columbus and his expedition, the king ordered his treasurer-general Gabriel Sanchez to pay 30,000 florins in gold to "his beloved councillor and

---

* "Vos fueron recibidos é pagados en cuenta un cuento é ciento é cuarenta mil maravedis que distes por nuestro mandado al Obispo de Avila, que agora es Arzobispo de Granada, para el despacho del Almirante D. Cristóbal Colón."

"Dió y pagó mas el dicho Alonso de las Cabezas (Tesorero de la Cruzada en el obispado de Badajoz) por otro libramiento del dicho Arzobispo de Granada, fecho 5 de mayo de 92 años á Luis de Santangel, escribano de racion del Rey nuestro Señor, e por el á Alonso de Agulo, por virtud de un poder que del dicho escribano de racion mostró, en el cual estaba inserto dicho libramiento, docientos mil maravedis, en cuenta de cuatrocientos mil que en el, en Vasco de Quiroga, le libró el dicho Arzobispo por el dicho libramiento de dos cuentos seiscientos cuarenta mil maravedis, que hobo de haber en esta manera: un cuento é quinientos mil maravedis para pagar á Don Isag Abrahan por otro tanto que prestó á sus Altezas para los gastos de la guerra, é el un cuento ciento cuarenta mil maravedis restantes para pagar al dicho escribano de racion en cuenta de otro tanto que prestó para la paga de las carabelas que sus Altezas mandaron ir de Armada á las Indias, é para pagar á Cristóbal Colón que va en la dicha armada." *Contradurias generales,* epoc. l, num. l18, in Navarrete, *Coleccion de los Viages,* ii. 5 ; *Coleccion de Documentos inéditos del Archivo de Indias,* xix. 456.   The above-mentioned Don Isag Abrahan is D. Isaac Abravanel.   The original manuscript has "Abraã," which Navarrete read "Abrahan."

escribano de racion Luis de Santangel."* This sum certainly included the remainder of the loan. Recent Spanish writers contend that Santangel received 17,000 maravedis as interest, but this assertion is wholly untenable. Luis de Santangel and also his kinsman Gabriel Sanchez† were the most zealous patrons of Columbus. Both acted unselfishly and solely for the welfare of their country. By their energetic efforts they succeeded in having Columbus recalled to the royal palace. At length his long-cherished plan of a voyage of discovery became a realized fact.

---

* Document dated Barcelona, May 20, 1493. *Arch. de la Corona de Aragon,* Reg. 3616, fol. 169 dorse.

† Gabriel's relatives, like all who bore the name of Santangel, were persecuted by the Inquisition. His father, Pedro Sanchez, was burned in effigy in Saragossa in 1493 "por hereje apóstata judayçante ; " and his brothers and sisters died at the stake as Jewish heretics.

CHAPTER VI.

"AFTER the Spanish monarchs had expelled all the Jews from all their kingdoms and lands in January, in that same month they commissioned me to undertake the voyage to India with a properly equipped fleet."* These are the words with which Columbus begins his journal. Without a word of disapprobation he thus mentions the tragic event which affected the welfare of hundreds of thousands, and which must have produced a profound impression upon the naturally vivacious explorer. His apathetic words are indicative of his fanaticism. This trait he did not, however, import from Italy, which at that time was a preëminently republican and commercial

---

* "Así que despues de haber echado fuera todos los Judíos de todos vuestros reinos y señoríos, en el mismo mes de Enero mandaron vuestras Altezas á mi que con armada suficiente me fuese á las dichas partidas de India." Navarrete, *Colleccion de los Viages,* i. 2 ; Las Casas, *Historia de las Indias,* cap. 26, i. 262.

country. A very different spirit was displayed by his countryman Agostino Giustiniani, the learned Bishop of Nebbio, who speaks of the Jews expelled from Spain with heartfelt sympathy.* He was the first to write a short biographical sketch of the explorer ; this sketch, which lauds Columbus, is given incidentally in the bishop's polyglot psalter, in the commentaries on the nineteenth Psalm. Columbus's religious enthusiasm soon degenerated into fanaticism in consequence of his contact with ecclesiastics—his truest and most useful friends— and in consequence of his intimate intercourse with men like the Bachelor Andrés Bernáldez† and Pedro Martyr d'Angleria, who boasts of the special friendship of Columbus. This fanaticism was also nourished by sordid avarice and the desire to promote his own material interests. In order to appear particularly pious, he even wore the dark-brown cowl of the Franciscans.

The expulsion of the Jews from Spain is closely connected with Columbus's expedition and with the discovery of America, not merely externally in point of time but also intrinsically. Not in January, as Columbus asserts in his journal, but

---

* *Annali della Repubblica di Genova illustrati con note dal Cav. G. B. Spotorno,* ii. 566.

† Bernáldez, the fanatical author of the *History of the Catholic Kings* was parson of the little town of Los Palacios. Columbus was his guest for a time.

on March 31, 1492, the Catholic monarchs sent forth from the palace of the Alhambra the edict that all Jews and Jewesses of every age should, on pain of death, leave all the kingdoms and lands of Spain within four months. The edict, which was signed by Ferdinand and Isabella, is of a wholly religious character, especially as regards the chief reason given for the act. The reason given is that, in spite of the incessant and most energetic efforts of the Inquisition, the Marranos were beguiled by those who adhered to Judaism to return to their old faith, and that this greatly imperilled the Catholic religion.* The Jews were generously allowed to take their property with them "by land and water," excepting gold, silver, coined money, and merchandise subject to the laws prohibiting exportation ; they could thus take with them only such articles as could be freely exported.†

The king and queen acted in full accord, but Ferdinand played the chief rôle in the barbarous expulsion of the Jews. Hence the edict was not

---

* The edict of expulsion is printed in full by Amador de los Rios, *Historia de los Judíos,* iii. 603 sq.

† The following words are at the close of the edict :— "E assi mismos damos liçençia é facultad á los dichos judios é judias que puedan sacar fuera de todos los dichos nuestros reynos é señorios sus bienes é faciendas por mar é por tierra, en tanto que non seya oro, nin plata, nin moneda amonedada, nin las otras cosas vedadas por las leyes de nuestros reynos, salvo mercaderías que non seyan cosas vedadas ó encobiertas."

signed by the Castilian secretary of state, Gaspar Gricio, but by the secretary of state of Aragon, Juan de Coloma, an old confidant of the king. Recent Spanish historians readily admit that Ferdinand was led to adopt this measure more by economic and political reasons, more by the desire to promote his own material interests, than by the religious zeal which actuated Isabella.* The king needed plenty of money to carry out his plan of bringing new territory under his dominion. He took it from the Jews, who were wealthy, especially in Castile ; some of them were worth as much as one or two million maravedis or more.† The Inquisition, which he had called into existence, and the expulsion of the Jews, which he had decreed, had one and the same object : the former aimed to secure the property of the secret Jews for the state treasury, the latter, under the cloak of religion, aimed to confiscate the property of those who openly professed to be Jews.

The Jews knew the avaricious Ferdinand and his secret plans. As in the case of the Marranos

---

* "La expulsión de los Judíos obedeció menos á causas religiosas que á económicas y políticas," says Abdón de Paz in *Revista de España,* vol. 109, p. 377. See also Adolfo de Castro, *Historia de los Judíos en España,* 136, and Bofarull y Broca, *Historia crítica de Cataluña* [Barcelona, 1877], pp. 377 sq.

† Andrés Bernáldez, *Historia de los Reyes Católicos* [Seville, 1870], i. 341.

when the Inquisition was introduced, so now those over whose heads the Damoclesian sword of expulsion was hanging, made an attempt to purchase the king's consent to the withdrawal of the edict. Don Isaac Abravanel—whose self-sacrificing services on behalf of the state were acknowledged and to whom the king and queen still owed a large sum of money, borrowed during the war with the Moors*—offered Ferdinand 30,000 ducats if he would avert the evil that threatened the Jews. Whether Luis de Sant-angel—then in friendly intercourse with Abra-vanel—or Juan Cabrero, or other Marranos interceded with the king, is very doubtful. They were, on the one hand, more or less concerned in the matter, and feared to lose their lives if they interfered ; on the other hand, they knew the king's obstinacy and avarice only too well. In fact, nothing could induce him to be merciful enough to recall the edict. On April 30, 1492, trumpets were sounded and the alcaldes publicly announced in Santa Fé and everywhere throughout the kingdom at one and the same time that by the end of July all Jews and Jewesses with their possessions should leave Spain, on pain of death and confiscation of their property by the

---

* See above, pages 77, 78.

state.* After that date no Spaniard was to harbor a Jew in his house or render him any assistance.

On April 30th, the very day on which the expulsion of the Jews was everywhere publicly announced,† Columbus was ordered to equip a fleet for his voyage to the Indies, and at the same time he received the contract which on April 17th had been arranged in Santa Fé between him and Juan de Coloma, the latter acting on behalf of the Spanish sovereigns.‡ Ferdinand, who had long energetically opposed the expedition, was

---

* " En último de Abril se pregonó con tres trompetas, Rey de Armas, dos Alcaldes, dos Alguacilles en el real de S. Fé sobre Granada . . . así mesmo de los reinos del Rey é de la Reyna, nuestros Señores, desde este dia fasta en fin del mes de Julio próximo inclusive, todos los Judios y Judias con sus personas é bienes sopena de muerte y de confiscacion para el fisco é cámara de sus Altezas. E este mesmo dia se habia de pregonar en todos los reinos y señoríos de los dichos Reyes, nuestros Señores." *Cronicon de Valladolid,* in *Documentos inéditos para la historia de España,* xiii. 192. Zacuto is in complete accord with this statement. In his *Jochasin,* p. 277, he says : "At the end of April trumpets were sounded in all the provinces and it was publicly announced that all Jews were to leave the kingdom within three months."

† Columbus's erroneous statement (see above, page 81) appears to be due to a slip of the pen ; instead of "January" we must read "April." He confused the proclamation made at the end of April with the expulsion itself.

‡ This agreement is printed by Las Casas, *Historia de las Indias,* cap. 33 ; *Documentos inéditos . . . de América,* xxix. 422 sq.

obliged to yield, thanks to Columbus's persistency, and was obliged to accept the explorer's excessive demands, which had twice caused the negotiations to be discontinued. He granted him the title of admiral, with all its privileges, and made him viceroy and governor-general of all lands which he might discover or acquire. Columbus was not content with dignities and honors for himself and his descendants. He desired also to derive considerable material profit from his voyages. The chief aim of his explorations was, in fact, to find gold, and in a letter to the queen he frankly declared that this gold might even be the means of purifying the souls of men and of securing their entrance into Paradise. Thus he stipulated that he was to have a tenth of all pearls, precious stones, gold, silver, spices, and other wares,—in short, a tenth of everything found, bought, bartered, or otherwise obtained in the newly discovered lands ; he was also to have an additional eighth of the profits of the present enterprise and of all similar ventures undertaken in the future, provided he should contribute an eighth of the expense.

Columbus now made preparations for his voyage. He went from Granada directly to the little port of Palos, which for some delinquency had been ordered by Ferdinand and his consort to equip two caravels within ten days. There he soon enlisted in behalf of his enterprise the services of the rich brothers Pinzon, who enjoyed a very high reputation among navigators. In Palos he also secured his sailors and travelling companions. The Jews, under the ban of expulsion, made preparations to leave the beautiful land which for centuries had been the cherished home of their ancestors, and to which they were passionately attached. They arranged their public and private affairs, tried to sell their real and personal property, and to secure the payment of their outstanding debts ; but only in a very few cases did they succeed in disposing of their property or in obtaining money from their debtors. As the day of departure approached, their sorrows increased. They spent whole nights on the graves of their ancestors, and they were particularly anxious that the cemeteries, which held the dearest of all their abandoned possessions, should be protected from desecration.

On August 2, 1492, which fell on the day of mourning for the two-fold destruction of Jerusalem, 300,000 Jews (according to some writers the number was much larger)* left Spain to settle in

---

* A rabbi, whose sagacity is extolled, "que llamaban Zentolla y al cual yo pusó nombre Tristan Bogado," informed Bernáldez that there were more than 1,160,000 Jews in Spain at the time of their expulsion. Andrés Bernáldez, *Historia de los Reyes Católicos,* i. 338.

Africa, Turkey, Portugal, Italy, and France. On that ever memorable day they sailed from the harbors of Cartagena, Valencia, Cadiz, Laredo, Barcelona, and Tarragona.*

---

* "En 2 de Agosto llegaron á la presente playa de Barcelona nueve fustas de gavia, entre ellas una nave del Tesoro y galera de Francia, y otros balleneros, y caravelas, en las que había reunidas mas de cuatro mil almas de judío los cuales se habian embarcado en Tarragona." Bofarull y Broca, *Historia de Cataluña,* 376.

> " Look, they move! No comrades near but curses ;
> Tears gleam in beards of men sore with reverses ;
> Flowers from fields abandoned, loving nurses,
>   Fondly deck the women's raven hair.
>
> Faded, scentless flowers that shall remind them
> Of their precious homes and graves behind them ;
> Old men, clasping Torah-scrolls, unbind them,
>   Lift the parchment flags, and silent lead.
>
> ' Mock not with thy light, O sun, our morrow,
> Cease not, cease not, O ye songs of sorrow !
> From what land a refuge can we borrow,
>   Weary, thrust-out, God-forsaken we ?
>
> ' Where, oh ! where is rest for thy long-hated,
> Hunted folk, whose fate in death unsated ?
> Oh! where is God?' So swelled the wail unbated,
>   From the mountains down unto the sea.
>
> Could ye, suff'ring souls, peer through the Future,
> From despair ye would awake to rapture :
> Lo! The Genoese boldly steers to capture
>   Freedom's realm beyond an unsailed sea ! "

Thus wrote the German poet Ludwig August Frankl in his *Christ. Colombo* [Stuttgart, 1836]. He was the first Jew who sang

On August 2d the Spanish Jews began their wanderings, and the next day, Friday, August 3d, Columbus with his fleet of three ships, the *Santa María, Pinta,* and *Niña,* sailed to seek an ocean-route to India, and to discover a new world. He was accompanied on his first voyage by not more than one hundred and twenty men (according to some writers, by only ninety), almost all Castilians and Aragonese ; many of them were from Palos, and some from Guadalajara, Avila, Segovia, Caceres, Castrojeriz, Ledesma, Villar, and Talavera— all cities in which before the expulsion large or small Jewish communities existed.

Were there any persons of Jewish extraction on the armada which under Columbus's guidance steered its course towards a new world? It was not easy for him to find men willing to accompany him on his adventurous voyage ; even persons guilty of crime were released from prison on condition that they should enroll themselves among the recruits. What was to prevent Jews

of Columbus's heroic voyage. His epic is dedicated to King Carlo Alberto as Duke of Genoa. [The translator of this volume acknowledges his obligations to Mrs. Minnie D. Louis for the English version of the extract given above.]

Another Jew, Baron Albert Franchetti, nephew of Albert de Rothschild of Vienna, has composed an opera entitled *Cristoforo Colombo, Opera in tre atti* ; the libretto was written by V. Penço, a Jew of Spanish origin [Genoa, 1883].

under the ban of expulsion, persecuted and home-
less, from taking part in the voyage? Among
the explorer's companions whose names have
come down to us—the complete list is lost—there
were several men of Jewish stock ; for example,
Luis de Torres, a Jew who had occupied a position under the governor of Murcia and who was
baptized shortly before Columbus sailed. As he
understood Hebrew, Chaldee, and some Arabic,
Columbus employed him as interpreter.* Alonso
de la Calle was also of Jewish lineage ; his name
was derived from the Jew's Lane, from which he
came ; he died in Española, May 23, 1503.†
Rodrigo Sanchez of Segovia was a relative of the
treasurer Gabriel Sanchez, and he took part in the
first voyage at the particular request of Queen
Isabella. The ship-physician Maestre Bernal
and the surgeon (*surjano*) Marco were also of Jewish stock. Bernal had formerly lived in Tortosa,
and as an adherent of Judaism, *por la Ley de
Moysen,* had undergone public penance at Valencia in October, 1490, at the same time as Solomon
Adret and his wife Isabel were burned.‡

When the fleet, whose crew was a very mixed

---

* Herrera, *Historia General,* dec. I, lib. 23.

† Navarrete, *Coleccion de los Viages,* i. 294.

‡ Inquisition records of Valencia, now in the archives of Alcalá
de Henares.

body of men—Spaniards, Moors, and Jews, as well as an Irishman and a Genoese—had covered more than two thousand miles, the seamen began to murmur loudly at the intolerable length of the voyage. Columbus calmed them as well as he could. On October 11th after the customary evening hymn, he admonished his crew to keep a sharp look-out for land. In addition to the gratuity of ten thousand maravedis offered by the king, he promised a silk waistcoat to him who should first sight land. At last, early on Friday morning, October 12th—the day on which the Jews expelled from Spain and their co-religionists in every part of the world were singing their hosannas*—the cry *"Tierra, Tierra"* ("Land, Land") arose from the *Pinta.*

In his journal Columbus confesses that land was first seen by one of his sailors ; but the avaricious explorer could not withstand the temptation to claim the royal gratuity of ten thousand maravedis, and the poor sailor lost this as well as the promised waistcoat. Who was the fortunate mariner whose hopes were thus shattered? Gonçalo Fernandez de Oviedo, who saw the Jews depart from Spain and heard their doleful lamentations, was informed (so he tells us) by Vicente Pinzon, the commander of the *Niña,* and by the

---

* It was "hosanna rabbah," a day on which the Jews recited many prayers beginning with the word "hosanna."

seaman Hernan Perez Matheos, that it was a sailor from Lepe who first saw a distant light and cried "Land." According to Oviedo, when this man found that he had been defrauded of the gratuity, he obtained his discharge, went to Africa, and there discarded Christianity for his old faith. The chronicler does not inform us whether the old faith was Judaism.* According to others, it was Rodrigo de Triana, a sailor of the *Pinta,* who first cried "Land."

The land was Watling's Island or perhaps Acklin Island ; the natives called it Guanahani. We are told that it was given this name by the Spanish Jews on board the *Pinta*, and Guanahani is even said to be formed from Hebrew words. A professor of the Oriental languages in Tacubaya, who comes from Mahón on the island of Minorca and who calls Isaac Abravanel his ancestor, claims to have been led to this etymological discovery by a Spanish ballad, which, he asserts, he received from Spanish Jews in Barbary. According to this ballad, in which there is a sprinkling of Hebrew and Arabic words, as soon as Rodrigo de Triana saw

---

* " . . . porque no se le dieron las albricas . . . se passo en Affricay y renego la fé ; " Oviedo, *Coron. de las Indias* [1547], cap. 5, pag. 7. "I asi el marinero de Lepe se pasó en Berberia y ali renego la fé ; " Gómara, *Historia de las Indias,* 168 ; Oviedo, *Historia general y natural de las Indias* [Madrid, 1851], i. 24.

land he uttered the little Hebrew word "I, I" ("Island, Island"), to one of his Jewish comrades. The latter then asked in the same language *"W'an-nah?"* ("And where?"). Thereupon Triana responded *"Hen-i"* ("There is the island"). Thus originated the name "Uanaheni" or "Guana-hani."* This childish explanation of the word is not worthy of serious consideration. Rodrigo de Triana was not a Jew, nor did he speak Hebrew, and Guanahani is known to be a word of Indian origin.

Columbus took possession of this island for the ruler of Castile, and then, sailing southwest to Fernandina, discovered the island which he named Isabella in honor of the queen. Still searching for the island of Cipango with its fabulous wealth of gold and spices, he reached Cuba by the end of October. He believed that he was in the immediate neighborhood of the Great Khan's kingdom, and he determined to send envoys into the interior to ascertain, as he expressed it in a letter to Luis de Santangel, whether a king or great cities were there. This mission he entrusted to Luis de Torres, who was accompanied by Rodrigo de Jerez of Aya-monte.† Columbus gave them specific instruc-

---

* F. Rivas Puigcerver, *Los Judios y el Nuevo Mundo* [Mexico, 1891]. See also *Boletin de la real Academia de la Historia,* xix. 364, and xx. 215 sq.

† Harrisse, *Chr. Colomb,* i. 421, 437.

tions, ordered them to prepare the way for a treaty of peace between the ruler of the country and the Castilian crown, and gave them a letter and presents for the former. They also took with them samples of pepper and other spices, in order to show them to the natives and ascertain where such things grew. On Friday, November 2d, Luis de Torres and his companion began their journey into the unknown land, and returned to Columbus on the sixth. They reported that, after travelling sixty miles, they came to a place with fifty huts and with a population of about one thousand persons; here they found men and women with fire in their hands, with which they lit one end of a small roll held in the mouth ; it resembled dried leaves and was called *tabaco;** they inhaled the other end of the little roll, and blew forth great clouds of smoke through the mouth and nose. The two envoys received a very friendly welcome from the natives and their chief ; the women kissed their hands and feet, and when they departed they were escorted by the ruler, his son, and more than five hundred persons.†

---

* "Hallaron . . . por el camino mucha gente que atravesaba á sus pueblos, mugeres y hombres, con un tizon en la mano, yerbas para tomar sus sahumerios que acostumbraban." Navarrete, *Coleccion de los Viages,* i. 51.

† Franc. Ad. de Varnhagen, *La verdadera Guanahani de Colon* [Santiago, 1864], pp. 31 sq.

Luis de Torres, the first European who discovered the use of tobacco, was also the first person of Jewish stock who settled in Cuba. He won the favor of the ruler, the cacique, and received from him as presents not merely lands but also slaves—five adults and a child.* The king and queen of Spain granted him a yearly allowance of 8,645 maravedis,† and he died in the newly discovered land.‡

In Cuba, Española, and the other islands which he discovered, Columbus found natives who had their caciques, and their own language and traditions. To what race did these aborigines of America belong? Several writers have asserted, and have displayed much learning in attempting to prove, that the aborigines were descendants of the Jews.§ This result was reached already in the sixteenth century by the Spanish clergyman Roldan ; his arguments were derived from an unpublished manuscript which he discovered in

---

* "Luis de Torres . . . en el dicho cacique un niño . . . cinco viejos que no son de servicio." *Documentos inéditos del Archivo de Indias,* i. 87.

† *Arch. de Indias,* 39, 2, ⅛. The allowance of Maestre Alonso *físico* was 11,188 maravedis.

‡ Ces. Fernández Duro, *Estudios auxiliares para reconstitución de la nao Santa María* [Madrid, 1892], p. 61.

§ Among other writers, see Gaffarel, *Histoire de la découverte de l'Amérique* [Paris, 1892], i. 89 sq.

the Library of S. Pablo in Seville.* Montesinos,†
who possessed the manuscripts of Luis Lopez, the
learned Bishop of Quito, was convinced that the
Peruvians were of Jewish origin. The view of
Roldan and of Gregorio Garcia,‡ that the aborigines of America were descendants of the Jews,
was maintained with many arguments in one and
the same year, 1650, independently by the Englishman Thorowgood§ and by the Portuguese Jew
Manasseh ben Isreal, a renowned rabbi of Amsterdam who induced Cromwell to allow the Jews
to return to England. A Portuguese Marrano of
Villaflor, who, strange to say, also called himself
Montesinos and afterwards assumed the name
Aaron Levi, informed Manasseh that he had
mingled in South America with Jews of the Ten
Tribes. Manasseh's book attracted much attention and was translated into Latin, Spanish,
Dutch, English, Italian, and Hebrew.‖ Nor has
interest in it ceased even at the present day ;

---

* See Appendix viii.

† He was a fiery and fearless clergyman, who for a long time
resided in Lima early in the sixteenth century.

‡ Greg. Garcia, *Origen de los Indios de el Nuevo Mondo*
[Valencia, 1607].

§ Thorowgood, *Jews in America ; or Probabilities that the
Americans are of that Race* [London, 1650].

‖ Menasse ben Israel, *Esperança de Isreal* [Amsterdam, 1650;
2d edition, Smyrna, 1659]. The Latin translation is entitled
Spes Israelis [anno 1650].

this treatise "on the origin of the Americans" was reprinted twelve years ago by the Spaniard Santágo Perez Junquera.* The descent of the Americans is, in fact, a question which has often been discussed since the discovery of America down to the present day. Even in recent times the Englishman Lord Kingsborough devoted his time, his attainments, and the greater part of his large fortune to the publication of a collection of American documents, in order to prove the Jewish origin of the Americans.†

It is not improbable that the Jews who were driven from Nineveh by Salmanassar wandered into uninhabited regions. According to Herrera, the Indians cherished the tradition that Yucatan had been settled by tribes from the Orient. Several writers give the exact route by which the Jews travelled until they settled in Cuba. Lord Kingsborough even asserts that they crossed Behring Straits, and then proceeded to Mexico and Peru.

---

* Junquera, *Esperanza de Israel. Reimpresión del libro . . . sobre el orígen de los Americanos* [Madrid, 1881]. Rabbi Louis Grossmann of Detroit, Mich., translated a part of the work into English, in the *American Jews' Annual* for the year 5649, i.e. 1889, under the title *The Origin of the American Indians and the Lost Ten Tribes* [New York, Chicago, and Cincinnati : Leo Wise & Co.].

† *Antiquities of Mexico* [London, 1830-1848], vol. vi.

Of more interest than the mode of migration is the question whether any analogies in language, in traditions, in religious conceptions, or in religious ceremonies justify the acceptance of this ethnological theory. Roldan's chief argument in support of his view is the language of the Indians in Española, Cuba, Jamaica, and the adjoining islands. He contends that it has many resemblances to Hebrew; in fact, he even calls it corrupted Hebrew. He asserts that such names as Cuba and Hayti are Hebrew, and that they were first applied by the earliest caciques, the chiefs or leaders (*Kasin*), who discovered and peopled the islands. The names of rivers and of persons in use among the natives are derived from the Hebrew: for example, Haina from the Hebrew Ain, stream, Yones from Jona, Yaque from Jacob, Ures from Urias, Siabao from Siba, Maisi from Moysi. The names of their tools, of their little canoes or *cansas*, the name *axi* for pepper, the name of the store-house for maize, grain, and the like, all point to the Hebrew language.*

Their rites and ceremonies, as well as their language, form one of the main arguments in favor of this theory of descent. Circumcision prevailed among the Indians ; they often bathed in rivers

---

* See Appendix viii.

and streams ; they refrained from touching the dead and from tasting blood ; they had definite fast-days ; marriage with sisters-in-law was permitted if they were childless widows ; wives were discarded for new helpmates. They also sacrificed first fruits on high mountains and under shady trees ; they had temples and carried a holy ark before them in time of war; they were also, like the Ten Tribes, inclined to idol worship.* All writers and travellers agree, moreover, that there were many Jewish types of face among the Indians, the aborigines of America.

The question whether the American Indians are descendants of the Jews, whether they are the offspring of "the lost Ten Tribes," has often been answered in both the affirmative and the negative,† but it has not yet been definitely settled.

---

* See Appendix viii.

† See, among other writers, Garrick Mallery, *Israelite and Indian; a Parallel in Planes of Culture* [Salem, 1889]; translated into German by F. S. Krauss [Leipzig, 1892]. For other works on this subject, see *Narrative and Critical History of America,* edited by Justin Winsor [Boston, 1889], i. 115, 116.

CHAPTER VII.

COLUMBUS'S RETURN—HIS LETTERS TO SANTANGEL AND SAN-
CHEZ — PREPARATIONS FOR THE SECOND EXPEDITION ; THE
MONEY OF THE JEWS UTILIZED — THE SECOND VOYAGE—
PORTUGUESE DISCOVERIES — VASCO DA GAMA AND ABRAHAM
ZACUTO — GASPAR DA GAMA — FRANCISCO D'ALBUQUERQUE
AND HUCEFE, OR ALEXANDER D'ATAYDE.

DELIGHTED with the success of his expedition
and with the great treasures of gold, silver, and
spices which he had found, Columbus began his
return voyage in January, 1493. He gratefully
remembered that Luis de Santangel had furnished
him with the means of undertaking his journey,
and hence he regarded it as his duty to send
Santangel the first glad tidings of his success—a
detailed account of his voyage and discoveries.
This letter was written in Spanish near the
Azores or the Canaries on February 15, 1493.
In it Columbus spoke of the great triumph which
God had vouchsafed to him, and stated that
he and the armada which the Spanish monarch
had placed at his disposal had reached the Indies
in twenty-three days, and that he had there discovered many inhabited islands.* He made a

---

* His letter to Luis de Santangel is printed by Navarrete, *Coleccion de los Viages,* i. 167-174.

similar report to the treasurer Gabriel Sanchez.
Santangel and Sanchez im-mediately forwarded
these letters to the king and queen, who were then
residing at Barcelona, and soon afterwards their
majesties received the explorer with much cere-
mony.
The news of the discoveries rapidly spread
through the greater part of Europe.* Gabriel

---

* Columbus and the Spanish discoveries early attracted the attention of Jewish writers.   The first of them who mentions the
subject is Abraham Farisol of Avignon, who, when nineteen years
of age, settled in Mantua, and thence migrated to Ferrara.   Here
he was appointed cantor of the Jewish community, and he also
devoted himself to active literary work.   In his leisure moments
he studied natural science and cosmography.   The accounts of
Columbus's discoveries which were first published at Vicenza, in
1507, in a collection of travels in the New World, served as the
basis of Farisol's work entitled *Letter on the Ways of Life.* It was
written in Hebrew in November, 1524, and was first published in
Venice in 1587.   It was reprinted with a Latin translation by
Thomas Hyde in 1691.   This work, which is a sort of general
treatise on geography, gives some brief notices concerning America,
and calls the discoverer " Cristofol Colombo, a Genoese."
This subject was studied more thoroughly by Joseph Cohen, a
son of Spanish exiles, who was born in Avignon in 1495. He was
educated in Genoa, where he practiced as a physician until 1550,
when he and his coreligionists were banished from that city.   He
went to Voltaggio, where he remained eighteen years, and then
settled in Costelleto in Montferrat.   He was eighty years old
when he died.   He translated into Hebrew the *Historia general
de las Indias,* by Francisco Lopez de Gómara, which appeared in
1535, and the second part of which contains *La Conquista de
Mexico y de la Nueva España.* The Hebrew translation is in two
books : " The Book of India," and " The Book of Fernando Cor-

Sanchez gave a copy of Columbus's letter to a bookseller in Barcelona, who had it printed in Gothic characters ; within a year two editions were published. Leandro de Cosco prepared a Latin translation, of which four editions were printed in the first year, 1493. In recent years several English and Italian translations of these letters have been published.* They will always

---

tes," or "The Book of Mexico." The translation which was completed in 1557, exists only in manuscript. See *Revue des Études Juives,* xvi. 30 sq. Cohen also deals with the Portuguese and Spanish discoveries in his Hebrew treatise entitled, *Book of the Chronicle of the Kings of France and of the Ottoman Grand-Dukes,* which first appeared in Venice in 1553 or 1554. It was reprinted in Amsterdam in 1733, and was translated into English by Bialloblotzky, under the title, *The Chronicles of R. Joseph ben Joshua the Sephardi* [London, 1834-36]. The passages relating to the Spanish explorations were reprinted by Dr. A. Kohut in *The Menorah,* xiii. 417 sq. Cohen ascribes the discovery of America to Amerigo Vespucci.

    * For Italian translations of both letter, see *Raccolta completa dellig scritti de Crist. Colombo . . . di Giov. Batt. Torre* [1864], pp. 214-229 ; and *Lettera in lingua spagnuola dir. da Crist. Colombo á Luis de Santangel, riprod. ed. illustr. p. Gerol. D'Adda* [Milan, 1866]. Both letters are printed in *Notes on Columbus* by H. Harrisse [New York, 1866], pp. 89 sq., 101 sq. See also *Letters of Columbus to Luis de Santangel,* 1493 [New York, 1864] ; *Columbus's Spanish Letter to Luis de Santangel, escribano de racion of the kingdom of Aragon, reprinted in facsimile, translated and edited from the unique copy of the original* [London, 1891] ; *The first Letter of Chr. Columbus to the noble lord Raphael Sanchez, reproduced in facsimile from the copy of the Latin version of 1493, now in the Boston Public Library* [Boston, 1891. Edited by Henry W. Haynes].

form the most remarkable memorial of American history.

In order to guard against the jealousy of Portugal, and to secure for Spain the lands discovered by Columbus as well as those that he might discover in the future, the wily Ferdinand appealed to the pope for assistance. At that time the papal throne was occupied by the Aragonese Alexander VI. The only good thing that can be said of him is that he treated the Jews magnanimously ; he was, in fact, commonly called "the Marrano," or "the Jew"* Though he was not a friend of Ferdinand, he issued his celebrated Bull of Demarcation on May 3, 1493, which aimed to prevent future quarrels between Spain and Portugal regarding the possession of newly discovered territory. This concession was granted to Spain for all future time, on condition that her rulers should strive to propagate the Catholic faith in the newly discovered lands.†

While Columbus was yet in Barcelona, rapid preparations were made for his second voyage. Ferdinand did not now lack means. According to his own statement, he had ascertained that

---

* Döllinger, Beiträge zur Geschichte des 16. Jahrhunderts, iii. 383 ; Valent. Nemec. Papst Alexander VI. [Klagenfurt, 1879.]

† This concession was subsequently modified by the Treaty of Tordesillas.

the Jews, expelled from his kingdom   "for the honor and glory of God," had left behind them money or its equivalent in real and personal property, as well as many debts which they had been unable to collect. According to a royal order of November 23, 1492, the authorities were to confiscate for the state treasury all property which had belonged to the Jews, including that which Christians had taken from them, or had appropriated unlawfully or by violence.*   On May 23, 1493, the admiral of the newly discovered islands and Juan Rodriguez de Fonseca, Archdeacon of Seville, who was supervising the equipment of the fleet on behalf of the crown, were ordered to go to Seville and Cadiz for the purpose of securing such ships, seamen, and provisions as were needed for the second expedition.† On the same day Ferdinand and Isabella signed a large number of injunctions to royal officers in Soria, Zamora, Burgos, and many other cities,

---

* The document, dated Saragossa, November 23, 1492, begins as follows : "Ferdinandus Rex delectis meis Jacobo Casafranca et Benedicto Ginneu salutem et delectionem. Tempore expulsionis Judeorum nostri edicti et imperii ad honorem et gloriam Majestatis domini facto ab omnibus Regnis et terris nostris intelleximus ab ipsis Judeis sub ipso recessu varias et diversas pecunias esse extortas," etc. *Arch. de la Corona de Aragon,* Reg. 3552, fol. 162.

† The document is dated Barcelona, May 23, 1493 ;   see Appendix ix.

directing them to secure immediate possession of all the money, precious metals, gold and silver utensils, jewels, gems, and everything else that had been taken from Jews who had been expelled from Spain or who had migrated to Portugal, and everything that these Jews had entrusted for safe-keeping to Marrano relatives or friends, and all Jewish possessions which Christians had found or had unlawfully appropriated. The royal officers were also ordered to convert all this property into ready money and to give the proceeds to the treasurer Francisco Pinelo in Seville, to meet the expenses of Columbus's second expedition.*

The large sums of money which had been taken from the banished Jews were thus appropriated by the crown. For example, several bills of exchange which Juan Bran, a Jew who had fled to Portugal, was to pay for Antonio de Castro of Toledo to Julian Catanes and Bernaldo Pinolo, were found in the possession of various merchants, and were confiscated by the crown. The proceeds, 4,120 ducats in gold, were deposited in the monastery of Las Cuevas by De la Torre, an officer of the royal treasury. On May 23, 1493, the king and queen requested the Count of Cifuentes to take the money from the monastery at once and have it safely transferred to the treas-

---

* See Appendix x.-xvii.

urer Pinelo, in order that he might use it for the equipment of the fleet which was to be sent to the Indies.* Juan de Ocampo, the Alcaide of Orueña, had in his possession gold, ornaments, clothing, and other articles, abandoned by a Jew who had fled to Portugal. A detailed inventory of this property, drawn up by the royal secretary Fernando Alvares de Toledo and signed by other royal officers, was sent to Count Alonso, a kinsman of Ferdinand and Isabella; he was instructed to take charge of the articles, to sell them, and to give the proceeds, by the end of June or at the latest by July 10th, to Pinelo, to help pay the expenses of the armada which was to be equipped "for the discovery of the islands and continents in the ocean."† In like manner and for the same purpose Bernaldino de Lerma was ordered to transfer to Pinelo the cash equivalent of the money, valuables, clothing, and other articles belonging to the banished Jews which the king's bailiff Juan de Soria, the wife of Diego Guiral, Antonio Gomez de Sevilla, Alvaro de Ledesma, and other had received from the goldsmith Diego de Medina of Zamora. Bernaldino received an order to deal in like manner with all the gold, silver, jewels, and

---

* Appendix x.

† For the decrees, dated May 20 and May 23, 1493, and the inventory, see Appendix xi. and xii.

various other things (specified in an inventory
sent with the order) which Rabbi Ephraim,* the
richest Jew in Burgos, had, before migrating from
Spain, left with Isabel Osorio, the wife of Luis
Nuñez Coronel of Zamora.†
Not merely the clothing, ornaments, and
valuables which had been taken from the fugitive
Jews were converted into money, but also the
debts which they had been unable to recover were
declared by order of the crown to be forfeited to
the state treasury, and stringent measures were
adopted to collect them. Several merchants in
Calahorra, Burgos, and other cities, namely,
Alonso de Lerma, Juan de Torres, Alonso de
Salamanca, Juan Alonso de Sahagund, and others,
owed large sums of money to the wealthy
Ephraim and to Benveniste of Calahorra, who
at the time of the expulsion was an inhabitant
of Burgos. Garcia de Herrera, an officer of the
royal household, was ordered to collect these
debts at once, as well as all other debts which
the Jews had left behind them within the territory of Burgos, or at least such of these claims
as had not already been paid to the *corregidor*
Garcia Cortés. In like manner Luis Nuñez

---

* In contemporary documents he is sometimes called Rabi
Frayn, or Rubifrayn.
† See Appendix xv.-xvii.

Coronel was commanded to pay to Bernaldino de Lerma, without further opposition or delay, the 4,850 ducats which his wife owed for houses bought from the Jews.* The above-mentioned inventories of the confiscated articles found in the hands of Christians or in the hands of Marrano kinsmen of the banished Jews† enable us to estimate approximately the wealth of the Jews, as well as the avarice of the Spanish rulers. Among the possessions of the Jews we find spoons, cups, bowls, kettles, pots, candlesticks, canes, all of silver, also silver and gold rings, pearls and corals, a surprisingly large number of silver bracelets, brooches, belts, chains, buckles, buttons, and head-bands.‡ In their boundless avarice the king and queen ordered not

---

* See Appendix xvi. For the order sent to Garcia de Herrera, dated Barcelona, May 24, 1493, see *Coleccion de Documentos inéditos rel. al descubrimiento de las antiguas posesiones de América,* xxx. 77-91: "Para Garcia Cortés corregidor de Burgos en rrempuesta de lo que escrebió . . . de las debdas que le ocurrian cerca de la cobranza de las debdas que dexaron los judios en la dicha cibdad e su tierra y en otras partes que quedó a cargo de cobrar a vecinos de la dicha cibdad."

† From the Marrano Iñigo de Ribas Altas, whose earlier name is not mentioned in the document, various silver articles were taken which belonged to his mother-in-law, a Jewess who remained in Portugal. See Appendix xv.

‡ The law forbade Jewish women to wear ornaments made of gold. See Kayserling, *Das Castilianische Gemeinde-Statut,* in *Jahrbuch für die Geschichte der Juden,* iv. 278, 331.

merely all the confiscated valuables and clothing
of the Jews to be sold, but also the threadbare
damask, velvet, silk, and linen coverings and
mantles of the *Torah* rolls, and the silk table-
covers used in the synagogues; they were all utilized for the equipment of Columbus's expedition.
It is quite certain that the measures adopted by
Ferdinand and Isabella for Soria, Zamora, and
Burgos were also applied to all other cities and
provinces in which Jews had lived. From the inventories which are still extant we may infer that
in cash alone—in the form of ducats, doubloons,
reals, castellanos, florins, justos,* and cruzados—
at least two million maravedis† were taken from
the banished Jews. If we add to this the proceeds of the confiscated bills of exchange which
came from Portugal, the large debts due the Jews
in Burgos alone which the crown collected, and
the proceeds of the many gold and silver articles,
jewels and gems, specified as sequestered, the sum
which the state treasury gained by the expulsion
of the Jews—reckoned simply on the basis of the
extant inventories—amounted to about six million maravedis. This was more than four times

---

* A justo is a Portuguese gold coin worth 600 reis ; a half justo
is called an espadin.

† In the time of Ferdinand and Isabella, 1 mark of silver =
2210 maravedis, 1 ducat = 383 maravedis, 1 doubloon = 490
maravedis.

as much as was expended on Columbus's first expedition.* To this sum must be added the two million which the Inquisition in Seville handed over to the Florentine merchant Juonato Beradi, who lived in Seville and who had been entrusted with the equipment of the armada.†

It is impossible to compute the enormous sums which the Inquisition wrested from the Jews and Moors, of which the state treasury gained by the expulsion of the Jews. Poor Spain! According to an order of May 23, 1493, it was from the money of the Jews that Columbus was paid the ten thousand maravedis which the Spanish monarchs had promised as a reward to him who should first sight land; and on May 24th he received an additional gift of a thousand doubloons from the same source.‡ As we have already pointed out, it was also with Jewish gold that the expenses of his second expedition were paid.

On May 28, 1493, Columbus left Barcelona to make the necessary preparations for his second

* Cf. Harrisse, *Ch. Colomb,* i. 396

† "Las Caraveles , que os escrivimos, havian de ir á Indias dara Juonato Beradi por los precios que vereis: el obispo de Avila escriuio á los Inquisidores de Sevilla que os diesen dos cuentos . . . y vaya muy presto que hay en Indias mucha necesidad." *Coleccion Muñoz (Biblioteca de la real Academia de la Historia en Madrid),* vol. 75, fol. 168.

‡ *Coleccion de Documentos . . . de América,* xxix. 492 sq.

great voyage, and he sailed from Cadiz for America on September 25th. He was accompanied by twelve hundred men, among whom there were, as in the case of the first voyage, several persons of Jewish lineage. The list of the crew has not come down to us.

Columbus discovered the islands of Dominica, Marigalante, Guadaloupe, and Porto Rico, and ultimately reached Jamaica; but he soon fell from the pinnacle of renown to which he had so laboriously climbed. The hidalgos who accompanied him were disappointed in their expectations ; the success attained was not commensurate with the great cost of the voyage. The rulers of Spain, the distrustful Ferdinand and the fickle Isabella, withdrew from him their favor, until finally he fell into disgrace. This was partly due to the discoveries which the Portuguese made about that time.

Columbus's success had encouraged the Portuguese to continue their explorations along the south coast of Africa, in search of the land of precious stones and spices and an ocean-route to India. The plan which João II. had formed to undertake a new voyage of discovery, but which his death prevented him from executing, was taken up by his nephew and successor, Dom Manuel, soon after his accession to the throne. The commander whom he appointed to take charge of the squadron equipped for this purpose was Vasco de Gama, a man of great determination, well versed in cosmography and nautical science. Before dispatching the flotilla, however, the king summoned his confidential astrologer to Beja, the royal residence, in order to consult with him once more concerning the plan of exploration. This astrologer was Abraham Zacuto, mentioned in a preceding chapter, who in consequence of the Spanish edict of expulsion of March 31, 1492, had followed his aged teacher, the pious rabbi Isaac Aboab, to Portugal, and had settled in Lisbon. Henceforth he devoted his services to the land which, at least for a while, hospitably received him and his Spanish co-religionists. On account of his extensive knowledge of astronomy and mathematics, he was highly esteemed by both King João and Dom Manuel. In 1494 João made him an honorary present of ten espadins in gold, or three thousand reis;* Manuel appointed him his astrologer, and had frequent conferences with him concerning astronomical and maritime matters. At King Manuel's request, Zacuto devoted himself with much zeal to the elaboration of a

---

* Ribeiro dos Santos, *Sobre algunos mathematicos Portuguezes,* in *Memorias da literatura Portugueza,* viii. 163.

theory concerning storms, and he indicated how ships could, without danger, make the voyage to the Cape of Good Hope and return in a comparatively short time.*

King Manuel showed his gratitude to Zacuto, and asked the latter's advice concerning the proposed expedition to India. The astrologer did not conceal from the king the great dangers which would have to be encountered in a journey to so distant a land, but he said that, in his opinion, it would result in the subjection of a large part of India to the Portuguese crown.† Zacuto's works materially facilitated the execution of the great plans of Vasco da Gama and other explorers. Da Gama held Zacuto in high esteem, and before sailing from Lisbon on July 8, 1497, conferred with him and received information from him in the presence of his whole crew.‡

During Da Gama's return voyage to Europe, while he was staying on the little island of Anchediva, sixty miles from Goa, a tall European with a long white beard approached his ship, in a boat with a small crew. He had been sent by his

---

* Gaspar Correa, *Lendas da India,* in *Collecçao de monumentos ineditos para a historia dos Portuguezes,* i. 261 sq.

† *Ibid.,* i. 10.

‡ Before 1502 Zacuto went to Tunis, where he wrote his valuable chronicle, *Jochasin.* He died in Smyrna about the year 1515.

master Sabayo, the Moorish ruler of Goa, to negotiate with the foreign navigator. This visitor was
a Jew, who, according to some chroniclers, came
from Posen, according to others from Granada.
Expelled from their homes on account of their
religion, his parents had migrated to Turkey and
Palestine. From Alexandria, which according to
some chroniclers was his birthplace, he proceeded
across the Red Sea to Mecca and thence to India.
Here he was in captivity for a long time, and
later was made admiral (*capitao mór*) by Sabayo.*

When the Jew reached the Portuguese vessels
with their flying bunting, he greeted the fleet in
the Castilian language with the nautical salutation,
"God bless the ships, the captains, and all the
sailors." Great was the joy of the Portuguese to
hear so far from home a language closely related
to their native speech. Great also was the desire
of the Jew to obtain news from his native land,
which still remained dear to him. Trusting to
the promise of complete security which the

---

* According to Damião de Goes, *Chron. de D. Manuel,* pt. I,
cap. 44, "era judeu de Reyno do Polonia do Cidade de Posna."
According to Barros, *Asia,* dec. I, lib. 4, cap. II, he was born in
Alexandria. Correa, i. 125, calls him "judeo granadi . . . este
judeo na tomada de Granada sendo homem mancebo desterrado ; "
this does not agree, however, with the Jew's own statement that
before the arrival of the Portuguese in Goa, in 1498, he had spent
forty years in prison. His name is unknown.

Portuguese gave him, he went on board one of their vessels. He was received with tokens of respect, and the sailors listened with pleasure to his reminiscences. His desire to prolong the conference led Vasco da Gama to suspect that he was a spy. On a signal from the commander, the Jew, much to his surprise, was suddenly seized, and bound hand and foot. After being disrobed, he was unmercifully flogged by two menials of the ship. Da Gama swore by the life of his king that he would have him flogged until he should confess the whole truth. To escape the torments of torture he finally went over to the Portuguese, and in order to save his life he promised to allow himself to be baptized. He was named Gaspar da Gama after the admiral, who acted as his godfather.

The Jewish mariner Gaspar, or as he is sometimes called Gaspar de las Indias, was taken to Lisbon by Vasco da Gama. King Manuel, who was much pleased with the newcomer and liked to converse with him, gave him rich presents of clothing, horses, and servants, and also granted him a charter of privileges.* As Peschel truly affirms,† Gaspar rendered inestimable services to Vasco da Gama and to several later commanders of the Portuguese fleet. He was a mariner of

---

* Correa, *Lendas da India,* i. 192.

† Peschel, *Geschichte des Zeitalters der Entdeckungen,* 575.

experience, well versed in languages and fully informed in all matters relating to India.*

In the year 1500 he accompanied Pedro Alvarez Cabral on his expedition to the East. This he did at the express desire of the king, who instructed Cabral to confer with Gaspar on all important matters. Cabral employed him chiefly as interpreter. Splendidly attired Gaspar negotiated with the King of Melinde, whose acquaintance he had already made when he was in the employ of Sabayo. By assuming the Moorish dress as a disguise and by pretending to pray like a Moslem, he discovered a rebellious plot of the natives of Calicut to massacre the Portuguese.†

From Calicut Cabral sailed southward to Cochin. Gaspar had advised him to do this. The Jew had expressed the opinion that, with favorable winds, Cochin could be reached in a single day. He had also informed the admiral that a better harbor and much more pepper and other spices would be found there than in Calicut.‡

At Cape Verd, on his homeward voyage, Cabral met the ships which had been sent from

---

* He also wrote an account of the scientific observations which he had made during his travels. *Paesi novam. retrovati* [Venice, 1507], cap. 61.

† Correa, *Lendas da India,* i. 163, 199.

‡ *Ibid.,* i. 209 sq. According to Correa, it was by following Gaspar's advice that Cabral discovered the coast of Brazil.

Portugal expressly to discover Brazil. Amerigo
Vespucci, who was on this fleet, hastened to
profit by the knowledge and experience of Gaspar
da Gama, the best-informed man among Cabral's
followers. Gaspar gave him the desired information concerning the situation and condition,
the wealth and commerce, of the distant lands
which Vespucci intended to visit. The latter,
it may be incidentally observed, never mentions Columbus and his discoveries ; he ignores
him as if he had never existed. But he speaks of
Gaspar in terms of high praise. In one of his
letters Vespucci refers to him as "a trustworthy
man who speaks many languages and knows the
names of many cities and provinces, who made two
voyages from Portugal to the Indian Ocean, and
journeyed from Cairo to Malacca, a province on
the coast of the ocean. He also visited the
island of Sumatra, and he told me that he knew of
a great kingdom in the interior of India which was
rich in gold, pearls, and other precious stones."*

---

* " . . . . uno uomo degno di fede, che si chiamava Guaspare,
che avea corso dal Cairo fino a una provincia che si domanda
Malacca la quale sta situata alla costa del mare Indico . . . il
detto Guaspare, el quale sapeva di molte lingue, e il nome di
molte provincie e citta. Como dico é uomo molto altentico perche
ha fatto due fiate el viaggio di Portogallo al mare Indico." F. A.
de Varnhagen, *Amerigo Vespucci ; son caractère ses écrits, sa vie*
[Lima, 1865] ; Humboldt, *Examen critique de l'histoire de la
géographie,* v. 82.

In the year 1502 Gaspar made another voyage to India with a fleet which was commanded by Vasco da Gama. He negotiated with the King of Quiloa, who was known to be cunning and artful. In Cochin, a few days later, he again found his wife. This woman, who was noted for her learning, had withstood all inducements to abandon Judaism.* When the first Viceroy of India, Francisco d'Almeida, went to take possession of his post in 1505, he accompanied by Gaspar and, among others, by the son of Dr. Martin Pinheiro, the judge of the supreme court in Lisbon. Young Pinheiro carried with him a trunk entirely filled with *Torah* rolls, which had belonged to the recently destroyed synagogues of Portugal. He intended to sell them in Cochin, where there were many Jews and synagogues.† Gaspar's wife negotiated the sale ; for thirteen *Torah* rolls Pinheiro obtained four thousand pardaos. When the viceroy heard of this transaction, he reproached Pinheiro in violent language, and then,

---

* "Gaspar . . . que em Cochym tinha huma judia, que fora sua molher, que elle nom pôde fazer que se tornasse Christã. Esta judia era grande letrada na ley." Correa, *Lendas da India,* i. 656.

† In 1504, when Isaac Abravanel wrote his commentaries on the Book of Jeremiah, he saw a letter, written by Portuguese merchants who came from India with spices. In this letter they stated that they had met many Jews in that land. Abravanel, *Commentaries on Jeremiah,* cap. 3.

after confiscating the proceeds of the sale for the state treasury, he immediately sent an account of the whole affair to Lisbon.*

Gaspar returned to Lisbon with Vasco da Gama in 1503. King Manuel, who still held him in high esteem, conferred upon him the rank of *cavalleiro de sua casa* in recognition of his services.

In a relation similar to that which Gaspar bore to Vasco da Gama, another Jew stood to Affonso d'Albuquerque, commander of the Portuguese fleet and governor of India. In 1510, when Diogo Mendes de Vascogoncellos was sent by the King of Portugal to help the hard-pressed Albuquerque reconquer Goa, he met a ship on which were two very rich Castilian Jews. Their destination was Cananor, and there Albuquerque became acquainted with them. In answer to his questions, they gave him detailed information concerning the kingdom of Prester John (who, they said, had a Jewish admiral in his service), and concerning the Arabian Gulf, the commerce of those regions, and various other matters. Albuquerque gave the two Spanish Jews many tokens of his esteem, and induced them to abandon Judaism, at least for a short time. One of them called himself Francisco d'Albuquerque, after his patron, whom he loyally

---

* Correa, *Lendas da India,* i. 656 sq., 900.

served as interpreter.* The other, whose real
name was Cufo or Hucefe but who called himself
Alexander d'Atayde, was a very experienced and
trustworthy man, who knew many languages,†
and hence Albuquerque appointed him his
secretary. He became Albuquerque's adviser,
his constant companion, and most intimate friend ;
and at the surrender of the stronghold of Ormuz
he rendered his employer important services.
He enjoyed the admiral's complete confidence ;
and when the latter, slandered by his enemies
and discredited by his sovereign, died in Goa
broken-hearted, Hucefe at King Manuel's request
made a journey to Lisbon. He succeeded in giving the king a better opinion of the great hero
and statesman who had been calumniated at the
royal court.

In Lisbon Hucefe was in danger of being
robbed of his property, which he always carried
with him in the form of gold and precious stones ;

---

* Albuquerque employed as interpreters other Jews who had
been expelled from the Iberian Peninsula, for example, a certain
Samuel of Cairo. Barros, *Asia,* dec. 2, lib. 7, cap. 8.

† " . . . . homem de muyta verdade e que sabia muytas lingoas,
e muy sabido em todolas cousas, e muy verdadeiro, com que era
muyto do conselho do Governador;" Correa, *Lendas da India,* ii.
134. "Hecefe . . . homem em que tinha muyta confiança, que
era homem de muyto saber em todolas lingoas e nas cousas dos
Mouros, e homem de muyto verdade, com que o Governador se
muyto aconselhaue;" *Ibid.,* ii. 177.

but he found shelter in the house of Garcia de Noronha, Albuquerque's nephew, whose acquaintance he had made in India. Garcia received him hospitably and manifested his esteem for him in the presence of the nobility of Lisbon. He soon left Lisbon and started on his voyage back to India. He proceeded to Cairo, where he again openly professed Judaism.*

---

* Correa, ii. 135. "E morto Affonso Dalboquerque vieram se pera Portugal em tempo del Rey D. Manuel, e daqui tornáram a India e da India se foram ao Cairo e se tornáram Judeos ; " *Commentarios do grande Affonso Dalboquerque* [Lisbon, 1777], pp. 269 sq. According to Correa, ii. 177, Francisco d'Albuquerque died in Goa, leaving a family of several sons.

In 1528, when Lopo Vaz de Sampayo was governor of India, the Turks sent a fleet to help the King of Calicut; its commander was called "the great Jew" *(o grã Judeu)* This Jew with his fleet also hastened to the assistance of Khair-ed-din Barbarossa, when the latter was attacked by the admiral Andreas Doria. *Documentos remittidos da India, publ. da Academia real das sciencias de Lisboa, p. R. Ant. de Bulhão Pato* [Lisbon, 1880], iii. 274.

" As to Coron, it was reported at Rome a few days ago that Andrea Doria was informed that the famous Jewish pirate had prepared a strong fleet to meet the Spanish galleys which are to join Dorias' nineteen." *Letters and Papers of the Reign of Henry VIII.,* vi. 427.

CHAPTER VIII.

THE reception which Columbus met with on his return to Spain after his second voyage was very different from that which had been accorded him in Barcelona three years earlier. The constant complaints concerning his avarice, arrogance, and cruelty had shattered his reputation. Queen Isabella, who ruthlessly ordered Jews and Moors to be burned, had instructed him to be kind and indulgent toward the Indians. But he treated the natives cruelly; he harassed them with fire and sword. By his domineering conduct he also aroused the enmity of Juan Rodriguez de Fonseca, mentioned in the preceding chapter, who afterwards became Bishop of Plasencia. In an outburst of anger he kicked and violently assailed the Marrano Ximeno of Briviesca, Fonseca's accountant. Hence Fonseca became the explorer's greatest enemy. By his arrogant and heartless conduct he also aroused the enmity of the ship-physician, the Marrano Maestre Bernal. The conspiracy of Porras in Jamaica fomented by Bernal and by a certain Camacho seriously affected the admiral's destiny.* Until his death, which took place on May 20, 1506, in Valladolid, the discoverer of the New World had to endure considerable ill-fortune. While in this distressing situation, he frequently asked his old patron Gabriel Sanchez to intercede with Ferdinand and Isabella in his behalf; he also turned frequently for help to Luis de Santangel, who had been his ardent supporter in the past.†

Owing to Santangels' unselfishness Ferdinand always remained his loyal friend, and bestowed upon him many distinguished tokens of gratitude, for his great services to the crown and state. It was out of regard for Santangel that equal rights were granted to the Aragonese and Castilians in the New World.‡ From his marriage with Juana, who belonged to the distinguished and widely-ramified Marrano family of De la Caballeria, Santangel had several sons and one daughter, Luisa. In the spring of 1493 Luisa married Angel de Villanueva, who was afterwards ap-

* Navarrete, *Coleccion de los Viages,* i. 348.

† Ibid., i. 335.

‡ Cesáreo Fernández Duro, *Tradiciones infundadas* [Madrid, 1888].

pointed governor of the county of Cerdeña.* The king gave her a wedding present of thirty thousand sueldos, "in recognition of the many services which her father, the well-beloved councillor and *escribano de racion* of his household, had rendered and was still rendering him."† Envy on account of this mark of distinction disturbed the treasurer Gabriel Sanchez. He intimated to the king that his services to the crown and to the state were as great as Santangel's. Hence his son Pedro, on his marriage with Maria del Jjar, also received thirty thousand sueldos as a wedding gift.‡

The highest mark of distinction accorded to Luis de Santangel, "in reward of the many great and notable services which he had rendered the king with untiring zeal and with great promptness and solicitude," was a grant made by Ferdinand on May 30, 1497. This grant exempted him as well as his sons Fernando, Geronimo, and Alfonso, and his daughter Luisa, together with their children and heirs, from every charge of apostasy. In this document the crown also granted them the absolute possession of all personal and real

---

* He was a nephew of Moses Pazagon of Calatayud.
† See Appendix v.
‡ The document is dated Torre Villas, May 10, 1494. *Arch. de la Corona de Aragon*, Reg. 3616, fol. 215.

property which should fall to them, to their children, or to their heirs during their life-time or after their death, and which might be confiscated by the Church or the state on the ground of any accusation of apostasy. Finally, the servants of the Inquisition in Valencia and elsewhere were admonished, on pain of paying a large fine, not to molest them, their children, or their descendants.*

Luis de Santangel and Gabriel Sanchez died one year earlier than Columbus. After the demise of Sanchez, which occurred on September 15, 1505, the office of treasurer passed to his son Luis, who held it till his death on December 4, 1530. On January 30, 1506, Ferdinand appointed as Luis de Santangel's successors his son Fernando and his kinsman Jaime de Santangel; each was to have a salary of 8,000 sueldos and the customary perquisites. The appointments were confirmed on July 24, 1512.† Soon after the king's death, however, Fernando was deprived of his office, and Pedro Celdrán was appointed *escribano de racion.* Hence Fernando felt constrained to defend his rights before the *Justitia*, the supreme court of Aragon.‡

---

* See Appendix vi.   † See Appendix vii.

‡ In 1506 he had received 3,600 sueldos for special services rendered to the crown. The document, dated Salamanca, January 8, 1506, is in *Arch. de la Corona de Aragon*, Reg. 3555, fol. 123.

At that time the jurist Luis de Santangel, who had been appointed deputy of the Zalmedina for the year 1492, with all the honors and rights attached to that position, was deputy of the *Justitia* of Aragon,* and Salvador de Santangel of Saragossa was councillor.† In 1517 the Aragonese tribunal decided in favor of Fernando.‡ With Miguel Luis de Santangel, who in 1586 was a distinguished teacher of law and an alderman of Saragossa, the Santangels disappear from the history of Spain. That country will always cherish and honor the memory of Luis de Santangel, the pride of that family and the prominent promoter of the discovery of America.

From the outset Columbus gave the newly discovered lands a decidedly religious or ecclesiastical coloring. They had been discovered for the glory of Christianity and for the propagation of Catholicism, and hence he desired that they should be inhabited exclusively by Catholics. Moors and

---

* See the document, dated Granada, November 26, 1491, in Appendix iv. " . . . Micer Luis de Santangel, lugartenience del Justicia de Aragon;" *Libro de Actos de Zaragoza.*

† *Libro de Actos de Zaragoza.*

‡ "Sentencia á favor de Fernando de Santangel escribano de racion cujo oficio le disputada Pedro Celdrán, anno 1517." *Arch. de la Corona de Aragon,* Reg. 3880, fol. 36.

Jews were not to be allowed to settle there ; even
the Marranos, including those who had been persecuted and punished by the Inquisition, were
prohibited from migrating to the New World.
Nevertheless, the first person who obtained the
king's permission to carry on trade with the newly
discovered lands was Juan Sanchez of Saragossa,
a secret Jew, whose father's loyalty to his ancestral faith had cost him his life. He lived in
Seville, and was a nephew of the treasurer Gabriel Sanchez; hence he was also frequently called
"Juan Sanchez de la Tesorería." In the year
1502 he received permission from Isabella to
take five caravels loaded with wheat, barley,
horses, and other wares to Española without paying duty.* Two years later, on November 17,
1504, when the queen was very ill in Medina
del Campo, Ferdinand allowed him to export
merchandise and other articles to Española,
and to sell or exchange them for the products
of that land. This favor was granted in return
for certain "good services" which he had
rendered the crown, and with the understand-

---

* "Capitulacion con Juan Sanchez de la Tesorᵃ por la Rᵃ en
Toledo, 12 Setembro, 1502 : Tesorᵃ podra llevar 5 caravᵒˢ con
300 cab. de trigo é 100 de cevada, 6 cavallos . .. é mercaderias.
Todo lo sacaron libra de derechos." *Coleccion Muñoz (Biblioteca
de la real Academia de la Historia en Madrid),* vol. 75, fol.
143.

ing that such services were to continue in the future.[*]

In spite of the stringent laws prohibiting emigration, large numbers of Spanish and Portuguese fugitives from the infernal flames of the *autos-de-fe* —nobles, men of learning, physicians, and prosperous merchants—soon settled in Española and on the other islands of the Indies. They tilled the soil, carried on trade, promoted industry,[†] and filled public offices. Hence already in 1511 Queen Juana of Spain was obliged to adopt measures against the secret Jews, "the sons and grandsons of the burned," who held public offices. Every secret Jew who, without the permission of the crown, was in possession of such an office, was to lose it, and was, furthermore, to be punished with the confiscation of his property.[‡]   This

---

[*] "El Rey. Por hacer bien é merced á vos Juan Sanchez de la Tesorería, estante en la ciudad de Sevilla, natural de la ciudad de Zaragoza, natural del reino de Aragon, acatando algunos buenos servicios que me habeis fecho, é espero que me fareis de aqui adelante, por la presente vos doy licencia para que podais llevar á la isla Española ques en el mar océano las mercaderías é otras cosas . . ." Navarrete, *Coleccion de los Viages,* iii. 525 ; Navarrete, *Coleccion de Opusculos* [Madrid, 1848], i. 106.

[†] Jews expelled from Portugal first introduced the cultivation of sugar from the island of Madeira into America. Antonio de Capmany y de Montpalan, *Memorias historicas sobre la marina, comercio y artes de Barcelona* [Madrid, 1779], ii. 43.

[‡] The decree is dated, October 5, 1511; see Appendix xviii.

decree also introduced the Spanish Inquisition into the newly discovered lands, and full scope was given to its nefarious activity. One of the first victims of the Holy Office in Española was Diego Caballero of Barrameda, whose mother and father (Juan Caballero), according to the statement of two witnesses, had been persecuted and condemned by the Inquisition in Spain.*

Many secret Jews from Spain and Portugal also soon settled in the Portuguese Indies, especially in Brazil. They were scattered along the whole coast of the Portuguese colonies, and carried on an extensive trade in precious stones with Venice, Turkey, and other countries.† As soon as they felt secure, they threw off the mask of dissimulation and openly professed Judaism. Hence it is not strange that, as in the mother-country—in Lisbon, Evora, and Coimbra—so also in Goa, the metropolis of the Portuguese dominion in India, the Inquisition was established, with jurisdiction over the Portuguese possessions in Asia and Africa as far as the Cape of Good Hope.

To prevent the emigration of Marranos to the Indies, the king, or rather the regent, Cardinal

---

* *Coleccion de Documentos inéditos rel. al descubrimiento, conquista y organizacion de las antiguas posesiones españoles. Segunda seria* [Madrid, 1885], i. 422.

† *Documentos remittidos da India,* iii. 495.

Enrique, issued an edict on June 30, 1567, which stringently prohibited them from leaving Portugal without the special permission of the crown ; any Marrano, however, could leave the kingdom provided he found a surety for at least five hundred cruzados, which were to be forfeited to the state if he did not return within a year. As this law did not prevent the secret Jews from migrating to the Indies to escape the oppressions of the Holy Office, a similar but more stringent edict of March 15, 1568, decreed that persons infringing this enactment should lose all their property ; one-half was to be given to the informer, the other half to the state treasury.* Captains of ships received strict orders to imprison all Marranos found on any vessel sailing to the Indies, and to deliver them to the governor-general.† Not until the Jews and Marranos in the colonies offered to pay the state the enormous sum of 1,700,000 cruzados, was the prohibition to migrate rescinded by the law of May 21, 1577. This law allowed them freedom of residence and of trade ; in the future, no one was to call them Jews, New Christians, or Marranos.‡

---

* The law of March 15, 1568, is printed in *Documentos remittidos,* iii. 510 sq.

† *Ibid.,* ii. 215 sq.

‡ Porto Seguro (F.A. de Varnhagen), *Historia geral de Brasil,* 2d edition [Rio de Janeiro, n.d.], 412.

Notwithstanding the great sums of money which they paid for the right to reside in the colonies, the persecutions of the Inquisition continued, and hence the Jews in the Indies soon became a source of serious embarrassment to the Portuguese government. They made common cause with the Dutch, who were at that time fighting for freedom, and they gave them financial and other assistance. In their zealous love of freedom they even equipped ships expressly for the Dutch. A letter of King Philip II. to Martin Affonso de Castro, Viceroy of the Indies, states that two New Christians in Columbo were in active correspondence with the Dutch, and that four or five in Malacca were giving the latter definite information concerning the military plans of the Portuguese. The Marranos of the Indies sent considerable supplies to the Spanish and Portuguese Jews in Hamburg and Aleppo, who, in turn, forwarded them to Holland and Zealand.*

---

* " . . . . os Christãos-Novos de Portugal e Hispanha ajudavan a D. Manuel para armar alguns navios de guerra junto com os dos mercadores que por todos fizessen copia de trinta velas, e n'ellas ir D. Manuel para que mandavan dinheiro a Hamburgo e Alepo, e d'ahi se passava a Holanda e Gelanda, e que os Chistãos-Novos d'esse Estado entravam tamben na dita liga, e que em Columbo havia dous que se carteavam com os Hollandeses, e em Malaca havia quatro ou cinco que os avisavam pelos moços que jam aos portos onde elles estavam por cuja via havia d'ahi muita correspondencia con ellas." *Documentos remittidos,* i. 106.

As soon as the Portuguese government heard of these transactions, the Viceroy of the Indies was ordered to adopt stringent measures against the New Christians who were thus allied with the Dutch. The law of March 15, 1568, was renewed, and the captains of ships received peremptory instructions to confiscate for the state treasury all the property of New Christians who should be found on their vessels, and to send them back to Portugal. If no ship happened to be ready to return to Portugal, these New Christians were to be carried to Goa, and were there to be retained in prison by the Inquisition until some ship set sail for the mother-country. The Inquisition was to deal in a similar manner with the Jews and New Christians who had already settled in the colonies; a number of them were to be sent back annually to Portugal, and thus the Indies were gradually to be purged.*

After the death of Cardinal Enrique in 1580, Phillip II. of Spain, in his greed for new acquisitions of territory, also brought Portugal under his sway. Not merely was Portugal added to Spain, but the Eastern Indies were also united to the Western Indies; Asia as well as America fell under Philip II.'s dominion. Spain was now at the zenith of her power.

---

* *Doc. remittidos*, ii. 195 sq., iii. 7.

Philip II. was the son of a daughter of the Portuguese king, Dom Manuel, and he was a grandson of that handsome Philip whose infidelity caused the insanity of his wife Juana, a daughter of Isabella the Catholic. Under this melancholy, tyrannical monarch the Inquisition renewed its nefarious activity in America. Tribunals of the Holy Office were established in Peru and Lima, and Jews and Marranos were consigned to the flames.

Among the first victims of the Inquisition in Lima was the physician Juan Alvarez of Zafra ; he was publicly burned as an adherent of Judaism, together with his wife and children and his nephew Alonso Alvarez. A few years later Manuel Lopez of Yelves in Portugal, also called Luis Coronado, met the same fate. He frankly confessed that he was a Jew, and he made no attempt to conceal the fact that he and his co-religionists had observed the Mosaic law and had held religious services in his house. Duarte Nuñez de Cea, a merchant forty-one years of age, also died for his religion. Before ascending the funeral pyre he confessed that as a Jew he had lived, observing the precepts of Judaism, and that it was his simple wish to die a Jew, as his ancestors had done. His example of religious loyalty was followed by the learned physician

Alvaro Nuñez of Braganza, who lived in La Plata, and by Diego Nuñez de Silva and Diego Rodriguez de Silveyra of Peru. New-comers from Portugal were persecuted with particular rigor. On one day fourteen such immigrants were arrested at the king's command, and their property was confiscated.* In the case of King Philip and his successors on the Spanish throne—- as in the case of their ancestors Ferdinand and Isabella—fanaticism had its root in the material interests of the state.

In spite of such persecutions thousands of secret Jews fled, during the sixteenth and seventeenth centuries, from the Iberian Peninsula to the Indies, and especially to America—to the New World, which was not merely a land rich in gold and silver mines, but also the land where the light of freedom first shone upon the adherents of Judaism.

---

* J. T. Medina, *Historia del Tribunal del S. Oficio de la Inquisicion de Lima* [Santiago, 1887].

APPENDIX LIST

I.

FERDINAND I. OF ARAGON GRANTS PRIVILEGES TO THE SANTANGELS (1415.) [Arch. de la Corona de Aragon,* Reg. 2391, fol. 28.]

II.

JUAN II. OF ARAGON ALLOWS THE SANTANGELS TO SEARCH FOR TREASURES (1459). [Arch. de la Corona de Aragon, Reg. 3368, fol. 77.]

III.

FERDINAND THE CATHOLIC GRANTS A PENSION TO THE DAUGHTERS OF JUAN DE SANTANGEL (1488, 1492). [Arch. de la Corona de Aragon, Reg. 3349, fol. 236 sq.]

IV.

LOUIS DE SANTANGEL IS APPOINTED DEPUTY OF THE ZALMEDINA (1491). [Libro de act. Del Ayuntamiento de Zaragoza, A° 1492]

V.

LUIS DE SANTANGEL'S DAUGHTER RECEIVES A WEDDING GIFT FROM FERDINAND THE CATHOLIC (1493). [Arch. de la Corona de Aragon, Reg. 3616, fol.207.]

VI.

GRANT OF FERDINAND THE CATHOLIC TO LUIS DE SANTANGEL AND HIS DESCENDANTS : THEY ARE NOT TO BE MOLESTED BY THE HOLY OFFICE (1497). [Arch. de la Corona de Aragon, Reg. 3654, fol. 72 sq.]

VII.

JAIME AND FERNANDO DE SANTANGEL RECEIVE OFFICES IN THE ROYAL HOUSEHOLD (1506, 1512). [Arch. de la Corona de Aragon, Reg. 3559, fol. 77 sq.]

VIII.

LOS INDIOS DE LAS INDIAS ISLAS SON HEBREOS. [Col. Muñoz, vol. 42, fol. 60 sq. ; en la Biblioteca de la real Academia de la Historia en Madrid.]

IX.

PREPARATIONS FOR COLUMBUS'S SECOND VOYAGE (1493). [Col. Muñoz, vol.75, fol. 159 ; Bibl. de la real Academia de la Historia en Madrid.]

X.

THE JEWS AND COLUMBUS'S SECOND VOYAGE. [Arch. De Indias, P^{to} I-I-II 2/9. Un libro de translados de las Cedulas y Probisiones de Armadas para las Indias del tiempo de los Reyes católicos, años de 1493 á 1495, fol. 2 vuelto.]

XI.

THE JEWS AND COLUMBUS'S SECOND VOYAGE. [Ibid. Un libro de translados, etc., fol. 20.]

XII.

THE JEWS AND COLUMBUS'S SECOND VOYAGE. [Ibid. Un libro de translados, etc., fols. 6-9.]

XIII.

THE JEWS AND COLUMBUS'S SECOND VOYAGE. [Arch. de Indias. See Appendix XVII.]

XIV.

THE JEWS AND COLUMBUS'S SECOND VOYAGE. [Ibid. See Appendix XVII.]

XV.

THE JEWS AND COLUMBUS'S SECOND VOYAGE. [Ibid. See Appendix XVII.]

XVI.

THE JEWS AND COLUMBUS'S SECOND VOYAGE. [Arch. de Indias. See Appendix XVII.]

XVII.

THE JEWS AND COLUMBUS'S SECOND VOYAGE. [This and the four preceding documents, App. XIII.-XVI., are taken from Arch. de Indias P^{to} 1-1-1 2/9.; Documentos inéditos de Indias, XXI. 418 sq.]

XVIII.

QUEEN JUANA AND THE MARRANOS OF ESPAÑOLA (1511). [Arch. de Indias, lib. I, fol. 120 ; Coleccion de Documentos inéditos. Seg. Seria (Madrid, 1890), V. 307 sq.]

INDEX.

Credits

Back cover photo of Meyer *Kayserling* from E. Neumann, Kayserling, Budapest, 1906.

Back cover Columbus engraving by Johann Theodor de Bry, 1595.

Front cover illustration Keith Dolittle, 2002.

Printed in the United States
6303